"There are many times tl
it comes from those who provide comfort with the comfort by which
they are comforted by God. The truth of God that has been
experienced in the life of another is a foolproof guide. Erica McNeal
has just this expertise from a life of perseverance in areas that may
comfort us all."

Tommy Nelson, Author and Pastor
Denton Bible Church, Denton, TX

"What do you do as you watch a friend face challenges you have
never faced? What do you say? How do you demonstrate love and
support? Erica McNeal has walked through multiple life threatening
challenges with grace and dignity. Along the journey she took notice
of words and actions that brought both comfort and unintentionally
brought pain. All of us will eventually have to walk through the
valley either personally or with someone we love. This book will
prepare you for that journey."

Ken Davis, Author, Speaker,
Comedian and Speaking Consultant

"The title of this book tells it all. Even God can use our deepest grief
for His ultimate good. If you are going through suffering, have gone
through suffering, or know someone who is, then this book will be a
tremendous guide and comfort for you."

Sean McDowell, Speaker, Educator,
and Author of GodQuest

"*Good Grief!* should be required reading for every pastor who wants
to truly minister to the people of their church!"

Kevin Baker, Senior Pastor
Martha Road Baptist Church,
Altus, OK

i

"Although the Lord promises in His Word we will encounter trials in this life, nothing could have prepared me for the day I found my sweet baby lifeless in his crib. *Good Grief!* gives people who have experienced loss permission to grieve, while clinging to the hope we have in Christ; the only One who can restore and heal a broken heart. When often no one has a clue what to do to help, *Good Grief!* provides ideas for meeting real and immediate needs to those who surround the hurting."

**Jen Rumley,
Child-Loss Survivor**

"As a fellow cancer survivor times two, I am honoured to support and endorse, the most amazing, Erica McNeal. This incredible woman, has faced cancer times three and lost treasured children, embedded in her heart and life. She has faced the odds, 'like a trooper'. Not only pushing on, but pushing up, up and away. Taking her lemons and turning them into lemonade, firing her gloomy clouds, and writing to change her world, she's making a difference. This book then is a gift from Erica's soul, read it, but don't weep, see her best, when all was almost lost. Tell your world about this amazing journey and see your friends and family be inspired also. I can't wait to hear more about Erica's evolving journey."

**Jodie Guerrero,
Health Consumer Advocate
Australia**

"As a seven-time cancer survivor, I have been asked so many times during these trials, "What can I do for you?" In *Good Grief!*, Erica gives solid and tangible ways to walk through these dark times with those you love and avoid those clumsy, awkward moments when we don't quite say the things we should."

**Karen Smith,
Cancer Survivor**

"I survived cancer. Sometimes I wondered if I would survive the comments of people who meant to be helpful. It can be difficult to know what to say or do when others are experiencing life's disappointments. This book will help you be a true friend to someone facing difficulty."

Diane Davis,
CFO of Ken Davis Productions

"I can honestly say that *Good Grief!* changed the way in which I interact with others during their difficult times in life. I am always there to help others, but I've never known what to say. Now I do. Before reading this book, I would have felt awkward relaying my sympathies to others, especially if that person was clergy. But I'm very proud to say that this book has taken that fear away. It is a must read for all!"

Melanie Jenkins, M.A.,
Psychology Instructor

"*Good Grief!* is a personal look at the challenges that face every relationship during the toughest of situations. Erica and her family have struggled in faith through experiences that most of us only consider in our worst dreams! Unfortunately, they've also been forced to deal with well intentioned, but inappropriate reactions to the grief they've encountered. This book is part of Erica's response! In it, she clearly presents concise recommendations for those of us who regularly struggle with keeping a foot out of our mouth. Her advice is timeless and can truly help anyone who is living life with those who have been, or are, living through a season of intense grief. I highly recommend this book for anyone who needs advice on how to react to tragedy in the lives of friends, family or coworkers."

Lt Col Matthew Vann,
US Air Force

"*Good Grief!* is a book that <u>must</u> be read! It comes straight from the heart and deals with the reality of pain and grief, but in a way that leads to hope and healing. It is a must for anyone looking for hope and meaning in our fallen world."

Dr. Doug Munton, Senior Pastor
First Baptist Church, O'Fallon, IL

"There is no better teacher than one who has learned through experience. In this book, Erica McNeal gives you and I a gift by openly sharing lessons learned in the midst of painful experiences. Lessons that will help us to better come alongside, and encourage those who grieve."

Tom Dawson, Pastor,
US Air Force Chaplain
Scott Air Force Base, IL

"Communicating Christ's salvation, love, mercy, and compassion is one of the greatest ministries we have as Christians. Erica McNeal has helped me engage in that ministry more appropriately with the information in this book, *Good Grief!* May it be a helper to you as well."

Jo Ella Roe,
Biblical Counselor

"Erica McNeal shares her journey with heartfelt passion. She writes not only from her experience, but connects with those who feel pain due to intense loss. Her godly wisdom will bring healing."

Dr. Joseph C. Grana II,
Dean of Pacific Christian College
Ministry & Biblical Studies

Good Grief!

Good Grief!

How to Create an Oasis When Life is a Desert

Erica McNeal

WestBow

PRESS

A DIVISION OF THOMAS NELSON

WestBow Press books may be ordered through booksellers or by contacting:

WestBow Press
A Division of Thomas Nelson
1663 Liberty Drive
Bloomington, IN 47403
www.westbowpress.com
1-(866) 928-1240

ISBN: 978-1-4497-3422-0 (e)
ISBN: 978-1-4497-3423-7 (sc)
ISBN: 978-1-4497-3424-4 (hc)

Library of Congress Control Number: 2011963003

Printed in the United States of America

WestBow Press rev. date 2/17/2012:

This book is for you my love:
Todd, you prayed me through my most difficult hours and have
loved me unconditionally. You have inspired me to find the beauty
from our ashes because you continually guided me towards our
faith in Jesus Christ. I love you!

Learn from the triumphs and tragedies of others.
Life is too short to experience everything yourself.

—Erica McNeal

Contents

Foreword

When we've suffered the loss of something or someone we love, grief is as natural as sleeping when you are tired or eating when you are hungry. It's a natural response to the breaking of attachments through the loss of a person, thing, activity, status, romantic relationship, or anything else that has become significant. Grief has the power to disrupt and disorganize one's total life. It is preoccupying and depleting. Generally, grief is a process and not a state. But most of all, grief is God's remedy for healing a broken heart.

The shock of a loss of nearly any kind is always tempered by a degree of denial, which helps us to function effectively. As Duc François de La Rochefoucauld said, "Neither the sun nor death can be looked at steadily." This is why grief is a process more than a state of being. And, of course, that process can either be healthy or harmful. It can be good or bad.

Erica McNeal's message in this wonderful book ensures that your grief is good as you travel along the difficult road of loss. In addition, Erica also offers invaluable insight and tangible solutions for those who surround the hurting, so that we can all learn how to better help our loved ones grieve appropriately.

And don't worry. You won't find empty platitudes here. Why? Because Erica McNeal knows about grief first hand! As you're about to see, she reveals her story without flinching! She opens her life for you in these pages. Why? To reveal just how good grief can be.

We assure you that this book will take you to a place of genuine comfort – a place where God can sooth your soul and heal your heart.

Drs. Les and Leslie Parrott
"Helping Others Build Healthy Relationships"
Best-Selling Authors and International Speakers
www.lesandleslie.com

Introduction

My life is a barrel of grapes, my soul the grape seeds.
I feel the pounding and crushing blows against my skin.
My flesh is broken, exposing the delicate fruit within.
I am under intense pressure.
I look around.
My life appears to be destroyed.
I am left to sit and ferment.
I stink and feel useless.
My broken skin barely hangs on.
Juice accumulates at the bottom of the barrel.

Time passes.
I feel alone, exposed, and broken.
Has the wine maker forgotten?
Is he there? Does he care?
I am about to drown when I see his face.
It is kind and compassionate; loving.
I feel hope.

Is he coming to rescue me? Will he stop my pain?
He walks to the barrel holding each piece of my broken life.
He gently extracts some of the juice. His touch is gentle.
The movement creates a restless desire for freedom; escape.

He softly tells me to trust him.
He is not finished with me yet.
He will continue to care for me.
But, it is not time.
I don't understand my purpose.
Why won't he tell me?
I cannot comprehend this grief!
Will I ever understand?

I often hear his voice.
It is calm and quiet.
I breathe in deep.
I know he is there.

He draws near and gently extracts more juice.
I feel his presence.
He makes me feel safe,
Filling me with a peace only he could provide.
It is time.
In excitement, I await my freedom.
I know he will put the pieces of my life back together.
He will fix my brokenness.
He will make everything okay.

But instead, I am poured out into a cylinder,
Exposed and vulnerable!
I thought my pain was about to end.
Have I not given him everything I can? He wants more?
I see a large press coming toward me.
I close my eyes and scream.

The pressure is intense, the weight unbearable.
Every piece of my life has been squeezed out.
Just when I feel my soul is about to be crushed, the weight is lifted.
He has controlled the pressure.
All that remains is my skin and my soul.
I look at the winemaker and see his smile.
I feel frustrated.
There is nothing left of me.
I am simply a shell and a soul.

The winemaker lifts me up and shows me what only he can see.
Each area of my life has been poured into barrels, too many to count.
Each one engraved with my name.
In large letters, I notice each barrel has the same inscription:

Relationships

Under the boldness of this word, are smaller letters.
The five closest to me read:
Cancer
Marriage
Child-loss
Family
Failed Adoption

I am stunned.
Amazed.
Humbled.
For the first time, I realize my life is not about me.
My purpose is not for me.
I was created for Him:
The Wine Maker.

His desire is to make me pure.
Not a single drop wasted.
To be used as He desires, as He sees fit.
My life crushed.
Every part of me meant to bring Him glory.
My soul unharmed. Protected.
His love is clear.
My purpose understood.

By the time I was thirty-two years old, I had already encountered more tragedy than most people experience in a lifetime. I've had to fight for my life; suffering through radiation treatments and nearly dying from chemotherapy to beat cancer three times. I've been tormented with life and death decisions, as I struggled over whether or not to intervene on behalf of my tiny fifteen-ounce baby girl born at twenty-two-and-a-half weeks gestation. And after falling in love, I handed a child I believed in my soul was meant to be my son, back to his birth mother when she decided to revoke his adoption plan.

Over the last seven years, I have spent countless hours in both physical and online support groups, wondering if anyone else feels the same way I do. I was shocked to learn that I was not alone!

The reality is that the worst pain in life does not always come from illness, child-loss, death, or even grief itself. Many times, the greatest obstacles to overcome through difficult times are the unintended hurt caused by painful words spoken and inactions by those in our support system that care for us.

From my personal experiences, I've compiled this resource guide filled with examples of the great support my husband and I received during our darkest moments and the harmful words that stunted our recovery. My hope is that if you have experienced a similar tragedy, you will find comfort in our experiences. And, if you know someone who has experienced a similar tragedy, may these examples give you the wisdom to speak encouraging and positive words, along with ideas of how to provide tangible support in times of great difficulties.

"And we know that in all things God works for the good of those who love him, who have been called according to his purpose."
—Romans 8:28

Chapter One

My Life Crushed

In 1999, I was diagnosed with a very rare form of cancer. I was immediately told there was good news and bad news. The good news was the tumor had a name. The bad news was not only had my doctors never treated a patient with this type of cancer before, they had never even heard of it! At this time, the cancer had only been found in the stomachs of men over the age of eighty. I was twenty-two, my cancer was found in my neck, and the last time I'd checked, I was not a man!

Then the news got worse. There was no standard treatment protocol for this kind of cancer, because, to the doctor's knowledge, it had never before been treated. This wasn't too surprising, as I cannot imagine many eighty-year-old-patients who would want to put their bodies through the tremendous toll of chemotherapy or radiation therapies. However, this information made me quite uncomfortable, feeling like I would become the treatment protocol guinea pig for this type of cancer.

After many different tests, the doctors had more good news and bad news. The good news was the cancer had only been found in one location and had not spread to other areas. But, unfortunately, the bad news was really bad. The doctors informed me that if after treatment, this cancer ever returned, I could only have two months left to live. With so many unknowns about this kind of cancer and what was causing it, the doctors expected it could come back highly aggressive. Since the tumor had already been removed through surgery, the doctors suggested a three-week daily dose of radiation therapy.

I quickly learned that receiving radiation to your head and neck area is no picnic! By mid-therapy, I had developed open sores in my mouth (kind of like cold sores) and constantly had a swollen throat. This made eating or drinking very painful and difficult. In order to eat, I would spray my throat with a numbing agent and allow a frozen popsicle to thaw in my mouth, only swallowing when absolutely necessary. Then, after my mouth and throat were numbed and frozen, I would have about five minutes to eat soft, bland foods before eating became too painful.

I was also constantly exhausted and depleted from my body working so hard to regain balance, while trying to maintain my school workload of nineteen college credits. Though three weeks may not seem like a very long time, the accumulative effects of radiation therapy can quickly take a toll on a person's body. I was so relieved when my treatments wrapped up and my body could begin the healing process. After six months of diagnosing and treating the cancer, the doctors were excited to tell me that this disease had gone into remission.

Dealing with these circumstances in my final semester of college completely changed my life, my perspective, and the way I viewed the world. I was shoved out of my bubble of invincibility and forced to come face-to-face with what I truly believed about God.

About four-and-a-half years later, in 2003, I was newly married to the man of my dreams when my cancer returned. Unfortunately, when I found out, my husband Todd was away on a military deployment in Qatar and not expected to be home for another three months. I did the quick math and believing I only had a few weeks left to live, I called him to find out if he could come home. I truly believed we would soon be saying our final goodbyes. He informed his commander of what was going on and was sent home one week later.

The next thirty days were filled with test after test after test; everything ranging from simple blood work-ups, to CT scans, PET scans, MRIs, and procedures with names too big to figure out how to pronounce in one office visit. In my opinion, if it takes twelve syllables for a doctor to tell me the name of a test, that doctor needs to drastically reduce the terminology to no more than three or four syllables. For instance, an esophagogastroduodenoscopy should be nicknamed the "e-diddy test." The doctor will already need to explain the test to me and why it should be performed, so I figure he or she might as well bring the verbiage down to my level and make it a little fun.

Once again, after all of the test results came back, we received good news and bad news. The good news was the cancer was not acting aggressively and was only found in one location. In fact, this was great news! The bad news was that these new doctors also had never treated a patient with this type of cancer before. They too, had to make an educated guess for my treatment plan based on my previous cancer therapy protocol. You know, the one where I was the guinea pig!

We decided it was best for me to undergo another round of daily radiation therapy for three weeks. This time the side effects were even worse and my body took a longer time to recover. Again, I went back into remission, while spending the next few months dealing with the emotional roller coaster of facing a disease with so many unknowns.

Our Girls

In 2006, our first daughter was born. My pregnancy with her was relatively uncomplicated and we were so excited to be first-time parents. Within just a couple of weeks after she was born, it felt like she had always been a part of our lives. We could not imagine life any other way. It has only been recently that we have learned what a miracle she truly is. In reality, she should not exist! She is now six years old, is the spitting image of my husband, and is a complete daddy's girl. She is amazing, has a very sweet heart, and a genuine love for other people. God has spoiled us immensely to allow us to be her parents.

Seventeen months after she was born, I was faced with making life and death decisions for our second daughter Kylie. I'd been on bed rest for four months and had gone into pre-term labor twice. When I called my husband to inform him I was heading back to the hospital for the third time, I asked him not to come. I fully expected the doctors would be able to use their triple threat of drugs and successfully stop my labor once again.

However, I was wrong! My labor had progressed too far this time. I was sitting in a hospital bed, contracting every three minutes, racing against time to make an impossible decision: my life or hers? It would likely be one or the other.

If I went by ambulance to another hospital forty-five minutes away, the doctors would have a one percent chance of saving her life. Seeking my doctor's guidance, I asked him to talk me through what kind of life we would be choosing for Kylie if the doctors were able to successfully save her.

He shared with me that the majority of the very few babies who survive at twenty-three weeks gestation endure brain bleeds, resulting in brain and possible organ damage. A baby born this early will also most likely face multiple major medical conditions including mental retardation, cerebral palsy, blindness, deafness, paralyzed vocal cords, under-developed lungs, stomach-related issues, possible life-long feeding tubes, and dangerous heart defects, along with many other long term difficulties.[1]

My other option, that I did not like one bit, was to allow Kylie to be born at our local, small-town hospital, where the doctors could do absolutely nothing for her. In this hospital, our daughter would have a zero percent chance of life barring a miraculous intervention from God.

To make my decision even more complicated, I knew that if I chose to be transported I would likely deliver our daughter in the ambulance. For most people, this would not be a big deal. However, I knew that if the doctors were correct about my medical condition, there was a good chance that I would die before we got to the other hospital. The doctors believed I had placenta accreta, a condition where the placenta attaches too deeply within the uterine walls. In my case, the placenta had likely attached to the scar tissue of my previous C-section scar line. With this condition, the placenta would most likely not deliver correctly and could rupture my uterus, requiring an emergency hysterectomy in order to save my life. If I were in the back of an ambulance, this surgery would not be possible.

However, I felt so strongly that if God wanted to give my Kylie life, who was I to take it away? Who was I to knowingly choose death for her? Therefore, I signed papers to be transported to the other hospital and prayed that I would be able to see my husband one last time. I wanted to let him know how much I loved him and how honored I had been to be his wife.

With the ambulance staff on their way to my room, everyone left and I found myself praying, "God, if the end result for Kylie will be the same whether I have her here or there, please let me have her now!" I hadn't even said, "amen" yet, when my contractions went immediately from three minutes to thirty seconds. Through God's strength alone, I felt completely at peace and knew I had to make the decision to call off the ambulance staff. I buzzed the nurse and asked her to send the doctor back into my room to deliver my daughter, just as my husband walked through the door. Kylie was born five minutes later at twenty-two-and-a-half weeks gestation.

She was perfect. Beautifully perfect, with her tiny hands, tiny feet, long legs, a little button nose, and tufts of dark brown hair. I think she would have looked like me. She was 11 inches long and 15 ounces—the length of a standard piece of paper and about the weight of a can of soup. Just after I whispered in her ear that it was okay for her to go be with Jesus, my little girl died in my arms. Kylie lived for eighty minutes and taught us that whether someone lives for eighty years or a mere eighty minutes, life is but a breath; a mere vapor!

That first night without Kylie was lonely. My husband went home to stay with our other daughter and I stayed in the hospital. The nurse had given me two sleeping pills to help me sleep, but they did nothing. I stayed awake all night long and pretty much laid out all of my cards before God. I told Him exactly how I felt about everything. I was still in shock mode, but I also felt sad, frustrated, angry, and depressed.

Yet, somehow in the midst of these dark emotions, I also felt hopeful. In the depths of my heart, I knew that one day I would be reunited with Kylie again in Heaven. Through my numerous tears, the song, "Hold Me Jesus" by Rich Mullins, played over and over in my mind. That night, it became clear to me how grateful I was to have a personal relationship with Jesus Christ. For, even in my daughter's death, I could find peace and hope.

To this day, I will never know if the doctors were incorrect about the placenta accreta diagnosis, or if God chose to intervene on my behalf. It turned out that the placenta delivered easily and I never needed the emergency hysterectomy.

I spent the following year dealing with extreme grief and guilt over the decision not to intervene on Kylie's behalf. It was very difficult for me to grasp that this decision was the right one to make. I also constantly questioned everything I did and didn't do during my pregnancy with her. I lived in an altered reality, struggling through misplaced anger for many months, and at one point I truly believed that I had killed my own daughter.

My body was incapable of keeping her safe.

It was *my body* that formed the blood clot that got infected and made her sick.

My body kept going into pre-term labor and ultimately gave birth to her before she had a chance to survive—so, how was her death not *my fault*?

Was this the reality as everyone else around me saw it?

No way!

Was this my (distorted) reality?

Absolutely!

These emotions were so intense and difficult to work through. However, by the love and grace of God, I was incredibly fortunate to have an amazing man of a husband, along with a few close friends, who loved me unconditionally through the darkest year of my life. Without them, it would have been very easy for me to spiral into a dark and deep depression.

Our Boys

Seventeen months after giving birth to Kylie, Todd and I miscarried early on in a new pregnancy and decided to pursue adoption. I was excited about international adoption, feeling like I could have more control (and those of you who have adopted internationally can stop laughing now). And to be perfectly honest, I was afraid of adopting domestically.

My fear was that a woman could choose our family, but then change her mind and ask for her child back. This thought completely terrified me after what we had experienced with Kylie. I did not feel like I could deal with the loss of another child, especially another child I would hold in my arms. After working through these emotions with God (and getting over myself a bit), we chose to trust what we believed God was placing on our hearts and pursued a domestic adoption.

Being a cancer survivor, I needed to be in remission for five years in order to adopt from the state we lived in. One month after hitting that mark we called up an adoption agency and six months later, we were naming our son "Joshua Todd" and bringing him home from the hospital. He was absolutely breathtaking! In fact, he rendered me completely speechless when I laid eyes on him for the first time. As the multitude of tears fell down my face and soaked his blanket, I could not believe this beautiful gift I held in my arms was going to be our son. I was so in love.

When he peed on me, it made me laugh. After everything we'd been through, it felt good to be peed on. When he projectile vomited on me, I couldn't have been happier. He was so worth the cleanup! We were completely enamored with this little guy and so excited to start our lives as a family of four. In fact, that first night, Todd and I stayed awake most of the night just to watch him sleep and to pray for him.

The next day, however, we received a phone call from the adoption agency and heard the four words from the adoption worker that completely shook us to our core: "She wants him back!" Instead of terminating her parental rights that afternoon, JT's birth mother decided she wanted to parent. We were completely shocked, devastated, and broken!

Clutching him in the adoption agency, I whispered in his ear the life verse we had given to him, found in Joshua 1:9: *"Have I not commanded you? Be strong and courageous. Do not be terrified; do not be discouraged, for the Lord your God will be with you wherever you go."* I never thought this verse would be so devastatingly perfect, for him, or for me to find the strength to physically let him go. I could feel my chest tighten, while my heart literally ached. Handing JT back to his mom was just as painful as handing Kylie to the nurse just after she died. Those were the two worst days of my entire life.

We were crushed, angry at the world, mad at God, and desperately struggled to understand what had just happened.

The next few weeks were a complete blur and nothing made any sense. We grieved not only this child that would never be our son, but all of the hopes and dreams we had built for our family. From the moment this woman told us that she wanted Todd and I to raise her son, *this* little boy became a part of every new hope and dream we had created.

Nothing anyone could say or do lessened our pain. Our arms were empty once again and we truly did not know whether we could continue down this adoption road. Every time the phone rang over the next thirty days, I frantically prayed that it was the adoption agency. I wanted to hear our social worker tell me that JT's mom had changed her mind again. When the doorbell would ring, our daughter would tear down the hallway screaming happily, "My baby is here! My baby is here!" – only to be disappointed every single time. We *all* wanted him back! From the moment he was gone, our family felt incomplete. Yet with each passing day, the reality would sink in a little bit more. He was not coming back!

We had to get away! We needed to leave everything that was familiar and go on what we called a "grief vacation". We met up with our best friends and all flew out to Hawaii, our happy place, in order to begin our healing process. There is just something about the warm sand, the waves crashing upon the shore, and palm trees everywhere you look, that can help bring a sense of calm to chaos. I wanted nothing more than to hop on a surfboard, paddle out into deep, blue ocean and physically feel the rush and power of God displayed through the waves He had created. Being in Hawaii was a breath of salty air and the perfect place for our family to begin the process of dealing with our broken hearts.

Though we had physically let JT go, we were unprepared to know how to emotionally let him go. This was an experience we'd never faced before. With Kylie's death, in many ways this part was easier. She died. While there were many days I lived in the land of "If Only..." with her, not a single one of those thoughts could bring her back to life. This was an easy concept to understand because earthly death is finite.

However, with JT, as far as we know, he is still alive. And, as much as we desire to be a part of his life and to have a relationship with him, we can't! While we still love him, he will never even know who we are or what he meant to our family. This is the hurt and living grief that we needed to start learning how to process and move forward from, because the broken relationship lives on. It is constant, not finite.

During this grief vacation in Hawaii, Todd and I threw caution to the tradewinds and became pregnant again, this time with twins. Emotionally drained, we had just begun to place our hope in carrying these two babies, when they too began to die. Before we could even let our family and friends know they existed, I miscarried once again.

In God's own unique way of letting us know that our pain did not go unnoticed by Him, the same day our babies died, the child that is now our adopted son was born. Only God could redeem what was lost in such a personal way. We were completely stunned when we learned that our son's birth mother had chosen our family to raise her son. In fact, I was so silent on the other end of the phone call that the social worker thought our call had been dropped. Needless to say, we were completely caught off guard.

Our only request was to wait one week before taking custody of this little boy so that his birth mother's parental rights could be legally terminated. I just could not *go there* again and desperately wanted to do what I could to protect our hearts. While the adoption agency agreed, three days later, we received a frantic phone call from our social worker. The foster family that was caring for our son had possibly contracted swine flu and we needed to take immediate custody of him, even though the parental rights had not yet been terminated. And by immediate, I mean, the social worker asked us to be at the agency within thirty minutes.

Not only was it a forty-five minute drive to the adoption agency, Todd was still at work and we hadn't even begun to pack. Within about ninety minutes, we finally arrived at the adoption agency and we were immediately introduced to a gorgeous little two-and-a-half week old boy. He was fast asleep and completely oblivious to any of our chaos. Immediately, he melted my heart. From the very first moment we held our son, we have watched God use his precious life to help us understand mercy and grace from a whole new perspective.

Our son is now two years old and somehow looks just like my husband and his un-biological sister. We finalized his adoption in May of 2010 and celebrated with a family trip to Disney World. It was incredible to be a family of four; just like we knew it would be. Loving *this little boy*, our son, has been an incredible honor and privilege for our family.

Our Drama Continues

Two weeks after this Disney vacation, I was eating a bowl of ice cream when piercing pains suddenly shot through my jaw line. And I knew! My cancer had returned.

On the one hand, we were completely stunned. On the other hand, we could only stand in awe and thank God that He had allowed us to finalize our son's adoption before the cancer came back. Had my cancer returned before our adoption was finalized, the state we adopted him from could have chosen a different family to raise our son because I would no longer have been considered to be in remission.

It took only one test this time to diagnose the cancer—a big, fat, jumbo needle placed right into the tumor, without any anesthetic. Yes, it was quite painful! Of course, I also had an MRI and a PET scan, as a follow up to the needle aspiration, in order to make sure that the cancer had not spread. I was very fortunate to learn that once again, my cancer appeared to have only grown in one location and did not appear to be acting aggressively. What a complete relief to our family!

Over the six-and-a-half years between my previous relapse and this new tumor, a lot of research had been done for this type of cancer. In fact, after seeing twenty-three different oncologists (part of the difficulty in moving around so much with the military), I had finally found two doctors who had treated this type of cancer in another patient (part of the *joy* of moving around so much with the military). Based on new knowledge, we decided the best treatment plan was for me to undergo a very specific targeted chemotherapy regimen.

My chemo nurse dubbed the drug as "Vitamin R" (for Rituxan), because most patients had only slight reactions during the very first infusion, with little-to-no long-term side effects. In fact, she called this chemotherapy a miracle drug and had been administering this treatment for many years. I was told there should be no nausea, loss of appetite, vomiting, weakness, hair loss, insomnia, fatigue, muscle aches, or any of the major chemo side effects found in many other drugs. Sign me up!

But, please keep in mind that this is me we are dealing with! Five days after my first infusion, I ended up in the Emergency Room. I was having full body tremors, difficulty breathing, chest pressure, and chest pain. Based on these symptoms, the doctors feared I was having a heart attack, a pulmonary embolism, and/or a stroke. However, the EKG, CT Scan, and Echocardiogram all looked perfect, so, the doctors sent me home. They had no idea what was happening to my body or why, but they did not believe my symptoms would progress into an emergent situation. (In hindsight, I am shocked that they did not leave me in the hospital overnight for observation.)

Two days after this ER visit, I was scheduled for another infusion of chemotherapy. My oncologist refused to give me any more of the Rituxan until he had done more comprehensive blood tests on me. On the one hand, I will admit, I was a bit agitated! I was concerned that prolonging another infusion would compromise my care and that somehow the chemo would be less effective. I remained in this mildly agitated state for another week or so, until the tests my doctor performed revealed that I was highly allergic to mice. Really? Who is allergic to mice? This girl, right here!

Since this chemotherapy drug was constructed through hamster ovaries, had my oncologist authorized another standard dose of the chemo, the drug probably would have killed me. For most people, the normal Human Anti-Mice Antibody level will range from 0–188. My level was 483![2]

Once we came to understand that even with additional allergy medications given to me before an infusion, Rituxan was not going to work for me, my oncologist suggested a different regimen of chemo. However, I told him that I was asymptomatic. I was no longer experiencing any pain and could no longer feel the lump, which was very obvious beforehand. I asked him to consider running another MRI because I was convinced the cancer was gone. I didn't want to put my body through any more drugs if I didn't need them. After doing a physical exam, he humored me, authorized the MRI, and was completely shocked a few days later to tell me that the cancer was completely, 100% GONE!

What should have eradicated me, completely eradicated the cancer in just one dose.

That's right.
One dose.
Tumor gone.
God rocks!

In a matter of weeks, as quickly as my cancer came, it was gone. Our family could see this experience as nothing short of God's intervention. And, as of this final edit, I have remained in remission for nineteen months now!

"For God so loved the world that he gave his one and only Son, that whoever believes in him shall not perish but have eternal life."
—John 3:16

Chapter Two

Why Me?

The most common question people ask me when they learn of my story, is, "Why you? What have you done to deserve this?"

And my response is always the same: "Why *not* me? What makes me immune to cancer or child-loss?"

It is all about perspective.

These tragedies forced me from a very young age to firmly decide what I believed about God and build my responses around that belief system.

Was God the almighty cosmic killjoy, using me as a puppet?

Or perhaps He was a stern judge, punishing me for my sinful nature.

Maybe He really didn't care about me or love me since bad things were happening in my life. If He cared, He could have prevented them, right?

Or was it possible that these trials in my life were breaking His heart just as much as they were breaking mine?

I chose to find the answers to these questions through the Word of God. I wanted to understand what God Himself had to say about what I was going through and how He felt about me. While it has always been so easy to pull Bible verses out of context to fit whatever response I wanted to have, I really dug deep to try and understand God's heart; not my own fickle emotions.

During my greatest need to know that the God I loved, loved me in return, I found great strength and comfort through His vulnerability displayed in the Passion Week of Christ. Through studying these Scriptures, I could clearly see that God was not a cosmic killjoy or simply a stern judge. He was a compassionate, loving, humble, and most importantly, *a relational God.*

God's love for me is so intense that He allowed His Son Jesus to not only die, but to *suffer.* While the death of Jesus is what enables me to have a personal relationship with God, what makes me sick to my stomach is to think about how extreme the suffering of Jesus really was. I cannot even comprehend this depth of intense grief and physical torture, because I have nothing to truly compare it to.

If God's sole purpose for the death of Jesus was purely to provide a way to restore our relationship with Him, the suffering did not need to happen. Yet, God reveals His desire to relate to our own human brokenness in such an intimate way by *allowing* such extreme agony. It was this very suffering that brought me comfort, knowing that my own heartache and pain paled in comparison to what Jesus did for me on the cross.

What struck me most though, was that God had all the power in the world to **stop** the suffering of Jesus from happening. But, He didn't! He could have easily chosen an easier and different way for reconciliation. God could have decided to sacrifice a goat, or an elephant, or a llama, and call it good. He could have made us say a riddle, or hum a melody backwards in order to reconcile our broken relationship with Him. He is God—He makes the rules! Yet, His decision of how to show us the depth of His love is humbling when you truly grasp the fact that He allowed and endured the greatest suffering known to man. What an intense, unfathomable love God has for me, and for you!

Understanding this concept forced me to the following two conclusions:

1) If God was willing to allow Jesus to suffer, why should I be any different?

2) If God was willing to allow Jesus to die for me, should I not be willing to live for Him?

I still find myself at this exact same crossroads every time difficult circumstances come my way. Do I allow myself to become embittered and angry that God would allow tragedy? Or, do I accept that we live in an imperfect world where imperfect things happen, and look for ways to glorify God through my circumstances?

While I would love to say that my first response has always been an immediate acceptance to my struggles, this is not the case. There has often been a process (sometimes a very difficult process) for me to get to that point. However, when I have chosen to accept that God is allowing these difficulties to happen in my life, I have been able to watch Him use my trials to build rapport with others who have suffered in similar ways. There is nobody that can understand the depths of grief and emotion like someone else who has experienced a similar pain.

I believe the greatest attribute of God is that He is a relational God. So, if I want to become more like Him, I need to understand that every detail of my life, whether good or bad, can be used to build relationships. I now understand the feelings and emotions of a cancer patient. I understand the external stresses that can invade a family. I understand the agony and grief of burying a child. I understand the devastation of a failed adoption. I understand the challenging emotions of infertility. I understand loss. So, when I choose to use each one of these experiences to come alongside other people who are hurting, rapport is built, because I can relate to what someone else is going through.

Often times, people feel alone in their struggles and trials. They feel like nobody else could possibly understand what they feel or why they feel it. And yet, the reason that so many people feel alone is because, as a society, we generally don't talk about the trials we face, our grief, or our difficult circumstances.

We often bear our pain in secret, as if ashamed by what we are going through. Potentially, we've been hurt in the past, or are afraid of what someone else might say or think. Sometimes, our emotions are so complicated that we have a difficult time finding words to express what we truly feel. Perhaps, we view our burdens as a weakness, instead of seeing God's strength in what we are facing. Our reasons are endless.

However, the truth is that when people use their grief and pain as ministry opportunities, it impacts the lives of those around them. Others who have experienced a similar pain don't feel so alone, and might even find the courage to begin their own process of healing. Additionally, a person may have already begun to grieve, but can be given the gift of renewed strength and energy to continue pressing forward. But, you know what else happens? The man or woman, who has chosen to use their difficulties to come alongside someone else, does not feel so alone either. His or her feelings and emotions are validated when somebody else can relate.

When this type of rapport is established, lasting relationships are built. And, it is through these relationships, that we are given unique opportunities to share the incredible love of our Creator.

There is a miracle that takes place every time I entrust my trials back into the hands of God and allow Him to use my experiences as He sees fit. Not only does God continue to heal the brokenness I feel from my losses, but, I am also able to find beauty from our ashes and purpose in my pain.

"Pleasant words are a honeycomb, sweet to the soul and healing to the bones."
—Proverbs 16:24

Chapter Three

Control

Through each experience I've faced, I was always able to maintain some semblance of control—and I like to be in control! I made the decision to undergo cancer therapy all three times, instead of rejecting treatment. I asked the doctors to do everything in their power to keep me pregnant when I went into labor at eighteen, twenty, and twenty-two-and-a-half weeks gestation. Ultimately, Todd and I had control over the decision not to intervene on behalf of our daughter, and to let her go peacefully into the arms of Jesus. And Todd and I physically drove to the adoption agency to give back our "almost" son, instead of heading for the Canadian border (which we momentarily considered).

While my husband and I had some control over different aspects of our journey, we had zero control over the responses of those people who cared for us. Through vulnerability, many family members and friends shared their feelings of complete helplessness as they grieved with our family. And through loving support, many people carried our burdens as we faced each difficult circumstance, shedding the light of Christ on our darkest moments. There were even a few people who got down and dirty in the trenches of our pain, boldly facing the heart of our grief, allowing us freedom from judgment. To these precious family and friends, we are forever indebted and grateful.

But, at the same time, there were also many comments that were very insensitive, spoken by people within our support system, who cared for us. At times, it felt like they were intentionally trying to hurt us, because we couldn't comprehend how they thought they were being helpful.

These Christian men and women—even pastors—unknowingly crippled our growth by the painful words they spoke.

One of my roommates at a Christian University told me that I was selfish because I wanted to rest after a full week of radiation therapy, instead of spending our weekend camping and hiking.

After seeing my family and friends love and support me through cancer, my best friend told me that she wished she had cancer too, so that other people would like her.

One woman aggressively asked at what point she could pencil me into her calendar, aggravated because I had so many doctor's appointments to attend.

Someone close to our family told me that our miscarriage was for the best, because there was probably something wrong with our child anyway.

Another person asked how many more babies I was going to kill, after my second miscarriage left me heartbroken by the death of another child.

And, one man—a pastor—angrily told me that I had no idea of the hell I put his pregnant wife through when Kylie died. His own son was born the day we buried our little girl.

"Do not conform to the pattern of this world, but be transformed by the renewing of your mind. Then you will be able to test and approve what God's will is—his good, pleasing and perfect will."
—Romans 12:2

Chapter Four

A Call to Be Different

One of the biggest hurdles Christians face is the stigma or label of hypocrisy. Can you even count how many times you have heard the following argument?

"The church is full of hypocrites
and that's why I don't go to church!"

People use this excuse all the time! I remember the very first time someone said these words to me. It was somebody I was very close to and I was quite offended! In fact, his words made me angry. I grew up in a loving church family; a church with an incredible pastor who taught the Word of God and challenged us to lead godly lives. Our church passionately reached out to our local community in many different ways and in my opinion, did what a church should do. This church was my baseline and all I knew.

However, after years of hearing this type of phrase and experiencing my own hurt from other churches and Christians alike, my perspective has completely changed. I am no longer defensive to comments suggesting that Christians are hypocrites. Rather, I wholeheartedly agree with the person who makes this type of comment.

The truth of the matter is, they are right—the church is full of hypocrites! Argument solved!

We are all sinners saved by grace.
We mess up.
We fall into temptation.
We put our foot in our mouth.
We do dumb things.

We sin.
We are imperfect!

We wrongly blame the church for Christians being imperfect.

It is so easy to walk into a church building and simply think that everyone attending the service follows Jesus and should be held to a higher standard—and in most places, that's just not the case. If a church is doing its job, the church will be filled with Christians and non-Christians, in various points on their journey, who are hurting, broken, and sometimes angry—searching for hope!

Our family has been severely hurt by people who profess to be Christians, through words, actions, and inactions. However, I have learned that when a non-Christian says something hurtful, offensive, or treats us poorly, we tend to let them off the hook for behaving "ungodly." As a Christian, we easily find it unfair to hold someone to a standard they do not profess to believe in.

However, when we are hurt by someone who calls themselves a Christian, the impact is so much greater, simply because we don't expect it. Our standard for these men and women tends to be perfection; something none of us could ever attain. We wrongly expect Christians to always say and do the right things, especially when we are hurting.

Our natural tendency is to automatically label anyone who doesn't live up to this (perfect) standard as a hypocrite. Instead, we need to remember that not only are they sinners (just like you and I), and on a similar journey of faith, but perhaps they have never learned *how to love well through difficult times.*

If, as a Christian community, we are not careful about the words we choose to use and we do not act on our faith in Christ, our response to difficult times are no different than those of a non-believer. We are merely blending into this world, adding to the perception that Christians are in fact, hypocrites.

Jesus called those who love Him to be different: to be salt, a light in this dark world, to be of the world, but not in it.

"You are the salt of the earth. But if the salt loses its saltiness, how can it be made salty again? It is no longer good for anything, except to be thrown out and trampled by

men. You are the light of the world. A city on a hill cannot be hidden. Neither do people light a lamp and put it under a bowl. Instead they put it on its stand, and it gives light to everyone in the house. In the same way, let your light shine before men, that they may see your good deeds and praise your Father in heaven." —Matthew 5:13–16

The following three ways can help us learn how to be set apart:

1) We need to recognize that while we all fall short, it is possible to be a sinner and to still be filled with grace.

2) We need to keep our standards of Christians at a biblical level, yet not expect perfection, out of ourselves, or others.

3) We need to become better equipped to know what to say and do when those around us are hurting, so that we can help our loved ones move forward from their losses, instead of inhibiting their journey.

"My grace is sufficient for you, for my power is made perfect in weakness."
—2 Corinthians 12:9

Chapter Five

Grace

During times when the absolute most grace was needed, there were many people who rendered us completely speechless because they didn't stop to think before they spoke.

There were days we allowed the answering machine to pick up because we didn't want to talk to anyone. Other times, my biggest need was to share every emotion I felt, even when it was verbal diarrhea. We struggled to be around other people because we felt completely misunderstood, many times afraid to speak of our emotions for fear of being judged. We were the first of our closest family and friends to experience these types of tragedies, so at times, it felt like nobody else could understand. And, of course, we didn't want to ask for help because we felt like we were inconveniencing others, with our natural unhealthy desire to be self-sufficient.

Unexpectedly, our traumatic experiences also brought to surface unresolved hurt and pain from our past, something both Todd and I were completely unprepared to deal with. Our emotions were, at times, so dark and difficult to understand, that it was near impossible to explain our pain to most people. Words never seemed to justify our true emotions. And words from other people that were meant to be loving and supportive often left us wanting to withdraw from the world for fear of being hurt, rejected, or labeled!

What our family needed changed constantly through our unpredictable journey of grief!

We needed people to be flexible with us.

We needed people to stop talking and to listen, even if they didn't understand.

We needed people not to be afraid to ask how we were really doing and find out how we were processing our emotions.

We needed people to allow us to talk about the death of our daughter and our failed adoption, and not change the subject if we brought them up.

We needed people to help us learn how to live daily, because living in the past, or the future, was unproductive and futile.

We needed people to recognize that not all cycles of grief are sorrow, tears, and pain.

We also needed people to laugh with us!

And, we needed grace.

As I have contemplated this constant struggle throughout the years, I eventually stumbled upon a realization that revolutionized my entire perspective:

Our family and friends were experiencing their own first-time emotions watching our family suffer through a pain they could not understand either. They wanted so desperately to help, but didn't always know what to say or what to do.

While my trials affected others greatly, my parents could not have taken radiation or chemotherapy for me. My friends could not have given their blood to run my numerous diagnostic tests or transfer my daughter Kylie into their bodies. And nobody could have given us the closure we needed to let the little boy that was "almost" our son go. My body had the cancer; my body was Kylie's home for twenty-two-and-a-half weeks; and our arms were the ones to hand JT back to his mom.

Taking my eyes off of myself, I began to look at how my trials affected other people. Not that I felt responsible for how they were handling what we were going through, but I began to realize that my experiences weren't all about me. Even though people didn't know what to say, they felt compelled to say *something,* and sometimes those words came out wrong—very wrong. But, instead of immediately pinning a hypocrisy label to their shirts or solely listening to the words they chose to use, I worked very hard to catch a glimpse into their hearts.

What was the emotion behind their words?

What were they trying to say?

Listening to the words of our family and friends with purpose, I was able to recognize that many times, their intention was love, though masking a pain and grief they didn't know how to handle or express either.

The first time I was diagnosed with cancer, I had no idea what I needed or what words would bring comfort. I only knew what was hurtful to hear. The same goes with facing Kylie's death and our failed adoption. I was in the middle of processing a grief that I had never experienced before; a pain I could not comprehend. All at once it felt like my world had come crashing down and I was helpless to stop it from happening. I felt emotions that were brand new (to me), feelings that were difficult to define, and I lived many days incapable of answering anything other than "yes" or "no" questions, or making simple decisions.

My mood could change quicker than a chameleon in a painted desert—there were good days and very ugly days. Yet, each moment was part of the windy road on my journey to find healing and purpose through my pain. And for someone who gets carsick easily, the quick turns and twists sometimes left me emotionally nauseated.

"The LORD is close to the brokenhearted and saves those who are crushed in spirit."
—Psalm 34:18

Chapter Six

So, What Can We Do?

In the heart of our grief, many of our family and friends asked the exact same question: "What can we do?"

And most often, our response was: "We don't know!" We honestly had absolutely no clue.

Many times it felt like people were asking us to give them a "honey-do list" so they could provide support. The problem was no list existed, not on paper, or in our heads. We didn't know what we needed and our loved ones didn't know how to help. There was a disparity between the two which created conflict and unmet expectations, on both sides. None of us knew what we were hoping for from the other person until our unknown expectations were unmet. And, unfortunately, there was a lot of unintentional hurt that was caused, as a byproduct of these unmet expectations.

However, on this side of our trials, through countless hours of researching and walking through grief with our own loved ones, I have gained a unique perspective of what a person might need in times of great pain, when nothing makes sense and everything is unpredictable.

I understand that each person is unique and not all of the following suggestions will resonate in each circumstance or within every relationship. You know your loved one better than I do. My intention is not to put "off-limit" signs on every comment that can be misunderstood. Rather, my hope is to provide insight into *why* some words (and sometimes even love), can be misunderstood from the perspective of the person who is hurting. I want to give you a window into the mind and thought process of the person who is struck with grief and loss, in order to show you *how* certain words can be perceived when your loved one is in the process of healing a broken heart.

I believe there are certain phrases we've been conditioned to say, not knowing how painful those words can be until we are the recipients. And while, at times shocking, I use real life examples from our personal journey! I tell you what people have actually said. In fact, most of the comments in the "Words That Can Be Misunderstood" sections were spoken to us *in the middle of our darkest moments*. I include them in this book to reveal to you the power of words and also to remind you that sometimes in moments of high stress, frustration, and miscommunication, it can be very easy to use words that can potentially leave a lifetime of emotional scars and damaged relationships.

My hope is to give you suggestions of what to say or do differently; to combine the best words of encouragement and tangible support we received, with the most difficult words we heard. My goal is to provide solutions for those who find themselves at a loss for words, or struggling to know how to help their loved ones move forward. I will dive into what words are often times misunderstood (and why), words that are encouraging, things to remember, how to become intentional through your actions to effectively communicate how much you care, and how to specifically pray for your loved ones.

"Do not let any unwholesome talk come out of your mouths, but only what is helpful for building others up according to their needs, that it may benefit those who listen."
—Ephesians 4:29

Chapter Seven

Facing Difficult Trials

Words That Can Be Misunderstood:

"God will not give you more than you can handle!"

This is a common Christian line that is intended for comfort, yet, contrary to popular belief, is not biblical or very comforting. In fact, most people quote this line as if it were an actual Bible verse. (It's not!) Unfortunately, this line often strikes a nerve with many people who are hurting because it is incomplete. While many Christians will add a phantom, "through Jesus Christ", many others will not. As is, this phrase can make one feel as though God is a puppet-master playing with their lives and emotions.

Believing in this line also takes the emphasis off of what only God can do and puts the emphasis on your loved one. It can create an innocent arrogance of, "Check me out! Look what God is giving *me*—look what God trusts *me* with." I have even heard someone say in response to this very line, "I wish God didn't think so highly of me!" In reality, the trial they are facing is not about God trusting them. Your loved one's trial should be all about him or her placing their trust in *God*!

It is my belief that this Christian phrase comes from an inaccurate interpretation of 1 Corinthians 10:13, which states, *"No temptation has seized you except what is common to man. And God is faithful; he will not let you be tempted beyond what you can bear. But when you are tempted, he will also provide a way out so that you can stand up under it."*

In the first thirteen verses of this chapter, the writer of Corinthians, Paul, is addressing *sin issues* (not common trials or tribulations) for the people of Corinth. He is warning them to avoid the *temptation* to repeat the sinful acts that are found in Israel's (at that time) recent history. He is asking these people to stay away from idolatry, sexual immorality, the desire to test God, and the complaining or grumbling that can so easily consume a person's heart.[3]

Walking through trials bigger and more difficult than anything we can deal with on our own strength allows God to not only be our Savior, but to be our Lord as well. God *will* allow us to be stretched beyond our human capabilities in order to show us our need for Him, to deepen our faith, and to show us that His strength is limitless.

"This must have been part of God's plan for you."

Do your best to stay away from quoting Jeremiah 29:11 and sharing anything about God having great plans when your loved ones are hurting. While intended for encouragement, these comments tend to frustrate people and can actually cause anger in times of suffering. Many people I have spoken with wish people would stop quoting this verse and talking about God's elaborate and amazing plans for their lives while they are in the middle of processing devastation.

The original Hebraic text for Jeremiah 29:11 actually says, *"For I know the thoughts that I think toward you, saith the LORD, thoughts of peace, and not of evil, to give you an expected end."*[4] When you look at this verse in context, you come to understand it with a whole new perspective.

In his Commentary, Matthew Henry offers insight to understand that this Bible verse is actually about the restoration of Israel, the coming of Jesus Christ, and the restored relationship between God and those who will choose to love Him in return.[5] Jeremiah 29:11 is *not* about God planning every detail, triumph, or tragedy in our daily lives with the expectation of giving you a great life, or to prosper you.

God's desire is not to make us happy, He wants to make us holy! Allow your loved one to find purpose through their trials when they are ready. They will get there!

"God has a plan for everything, you just need to trust Him!"

God's original design and plan was perfection. He created a perfect world – a world we no longer live in, due to the consequence of Adam and Eve's decision to disobey God and sin.[6] We now live in an imperfect world where imperfect things happen. Sometimes, trials and pain are a result of these consequences and the curse of Adam and Eve, not necessarily because God purposed or planned for them to occur!

I have come to learn that there is a big difference between what God *plans* and what He *allows* to happen. While I do not believe that God planned or purposed for my cancer or child-loss from the beginning of time, I do trust that He is Sovereign. To say that God plans or purposes everything that happens in people's lives, states that God also plans or purposes things like rape or murder. While God is incapable of purposing such evil, He is absolutely capable and big enough to work in and through these types of circumstances.

That being said, I do trust there is absolutely nothing that has happened in my life that has not first been filtered through the hands of God. He is not surprised by any of my life's circumstances. When I choose to be open and obedient through even my deepest suffering, God can use my heartache, to not only make me more like Him, but to show His goodness to others. It is this understanding that allows me to continue to trust Him when bad things happen in my life.

"Let go and let God!"

This is another line that is rarely received as encouragement. Emotions from your loved one's trial will need to be processed in order to get to the heart of what they are going through. He or she needs to learn how to deal with his or her pain and their new circumstances. They are not able to just let go and carry on as if nothing has changed. A line like this can make someone feel as though they are not allowed to grieve or truly explore the emotions they are processing. Yet, accepting their circumstances and coming to grips with their feelings are very important steps in progressing through and overcoming their trials.

"I understand how you feel."

Even if you have experienced something similar to your loved one, each person is unique and deals with grief differently. Instead, consider saying, "I imagine you are feeling (frustrated, angry, distraught, confused, etc). Is that true?"

"When I went through this…"

Make your loved one's pain and grief about them, not you. If you are close, they will likely know that you have been through a similar experience and may seek your wisdom and guidance when they are ready. It is certainly okay to ask if you can share what you have been through, but please don't make statements that assume your loved one is ready to hear all of the details of the tragedy you have faced.

If you are not close, or you know that your loved one is unaware of your personal experiences, consider saying, "When you are ready, I've experienced something similar. If you'd like to talk, I'm happy to share my story with you." This gives your loved one permission to ask you to share your experiences at a later date, without causing him or her to feel pressured to listen right now.

There will be times when the last thing your loved one wants to hear is another story of someone else who has experienced loss. On the other hand, there will be times when hearing these same stories can bring healing. Personal experiences from others can give your loved one the confidence to know that he or she is not alone. They can also fill your loved one with hope, by believing in the possibility that they too, will be able to survive a similar grief. However, which way a person will receive your story, will often depend on whether or not your loved one is ready to hear it.

"Call if you need anything."

How many times have you asked someone who is hurting to call if they need anything? I used to say this *all the time* and thought that I was being helpful. However, nobody would ever call. The fact is that most people are not going to pick up the phone to ask for help because they will feel like they are inconveniencing you, regardless of how much help they need.

People don't like to admit they need help. We all want to be self-sufficient and not feel like we are being a burden to others. Call your loved one and offer to do something tangible or specific and give a date and time that would work for you. Take out as much of the decision-making process for your loved one as possible and make it easy for him or her to say "yes". Your loved one is exhausted in so many different ways and may only be able to make "yes" or "no" decisions at this time.

"Everything happens for a reason."

This type of comment is an empty platitude that means nothing. If you are unable to explain the reason for your loved one's trial (which is very likely), do your best to stay away from this phrase. In many circumstances, there are no good explanations for pain. And while, at some point your loved one might find purpose through what he or she has been through, that still does not mean their trial happened for a specific reason. This line is ambiguous and can create anger, causing people want to shout back: "Then tell me the reason!"

Avoid any statements that begin with: "you should", "you need to", or "you shouldn't."

Using these types of words immediately puts people in a defensive position and is likely to either shut down communication or leave your loved one feeling frustrated that someone else is telling them what to do. Instead, create conversations to understand how he or she desires to move forward by saying, "Talk to me about the options you are considering." Or, "Walk me through your thought process of what you think is best."

These phrases will hopefully open up a discussion where your loved one is more likely to share deeper emotions and consider your ideas. It is absolutely okay to offer suggestions, just be careful that you are not pushing your thoughts (or any agenda) on them. If they feel you are doing this, they may become defensive. Let your loved one talk and do your best to refrain from trying to "fix" their problem. Listen and be a friend. Often times, that's all they need.

Words That Encourage:

"What can I specifically pray for?"

"I cannot comprehend how difficult this is for you. What can I do to make life a little easier right now?"

Your loved ones may have no clue, or they may have a laundry list of things they need done. Personally do what you can and enlist others to take care of things you can't. Follow up and make sure their needs have been met.

"What do you need from me right now?"

Be prepared that your loved one may request some space and please do your best not to get your feelings hurt if/when this happens. Your loved one will need some time to work through his or her emotions. Make a note on your calendar to check back with him or her in a week, and then try again.

"I cannot imagine how devastated you are right now!"

When you e-mail, text, or call, say, "Don't feel like you need to respond, I just wanted you to know that I am thinking of and praying for you!"

This is all they need to know. It is so important for your loved one not to feel pressured to return every phone call or e-mail they receive. Letting people know you do not expect a response can take away this pressure while still showing that you care.

"It's okay to cry."

"Sometimes we just go through things that don't make any sense!"

"How are you processing and dealing with everything?"

Use words like, "What I hear you saying is..."

Think the best about your loved one! Clarify comments or conversations that you don't understand. It is very easy for words to have multiple meanings, or to cause confusion, especially when the process of grief is so confusing. Do your best not to jump to conclusions.

"I am sorry."

This one is tricky. For many people, it is comforting, as it can imply you are filled with sorrow for what they are going through. For me, it made me feel awkward because I felt like people were apologizing for my trials, which were not their fault. In fact, someone I knew was struggling immensely and against my better judgment, I told her that I was sorry. Her response, "I cannot accept your apology!"

"It's okay to give yourself some grace!"

There are some people who will give grace to everyone else, but rarely themselves!

"Be patient and give yourself time to heal."

"I would love to make your family a meal (or if you are long-distance, order some food for delivery). What sounds good?"

"I am making a double batch of our dinner tonight, can I bring one over for your family?"

Sometimes presenting the offer to provide a meal in this manner can make the recipient feel like it is less work for you (and in some ways, it is). This is great because many people who are going through difficulties don't like to feel like they are putting other people out or being a burden. So, in a sense, if you are already making a meal, they will likely feel like less of a burden and may be more open to taking you up on the offer.

"Please don't feel like you need to clean up the house or take a shower when I come over. If it makes you feel better, I won't shower either!"

"We live in an imperfect world, so sometimes imperfect things happen. And, it stinks!"

"Are you just venting or are you looking for my opinion?"

At any given moment, a million thoughts might be brewing in the mind of your loved one, ready to explode without warning. Sometimes, saying words out loud can be incredibly freeing (when it is not met with a judgmental response). Finally verbalizing what someone has been holding onto for so long can feel like a tremendous weight off his or her shoulders, even if their words don't make sense to anyone else. If you have not been through a similar trauma, do not expect that you will be able to understand, you won't.

Many times people who are grieving or hurting just need to vent! Asking if they are looking for your opinion shows them that you are not trying to fix their problem, but rather open to just listening, if that is what they need.

"There is no particular way you should feel or things you should do right now. What you feel today will likely be different than what you feel tomorrow and that's okay!"

"I don't know what to say, but I love you!"

This type of honesty will go a long way and will mean a lot to your loved one. You don't need to have all of the perfect words to say, because honestly, your loved one doesn't have them either, nor do they expect it.

A few more things to remember:

- There is good news and bad news when dealing with difficult times. The bad news is that you, dear reader, are not perfect. The good news is that your loved one is not perfect either. Keeping this in mind when you help your loved one navigate their trials will help keep your heart in check and your pride low when their responses are difficult to manage. Dealing with difficult times is a trial and error process for all people involved and mistakes will absolutely be made.

- Keep in mind that telling someone else about tragic events that have taken place is incredibly difficult. Put yourself in your loved one's shoes. How do you tell someone close to you that there has been a death, a separation, a massive car accident, a chronic illness, or a devastating diagnosis, when you know that the words you use will devastate someone else? It is never easy to be the bearer of bad news.

- Remember that the needs of the family extend beyond the initial offers to help and beyond the first few days or weeks of the traumatic event or diagnosis. Most of the support our family received happened immediately and over the next couple of days after we announced the relapses with cancer and child-loss. Once we were a couple of weeks out from dealing with these trials, most people had already stopped checking in with us to find how we were doing. It felt like life had moved forward for everybody else but us.

- Part of what is so unpredictable about grief is that the onset of any trauma can cause many different, and seemingly unrelated emotional triggers. The loss itself can bring up repressed memories, childhood hurts, conflict from broken relationships, self-esteem issues, unresolved past trauma or sins, unspoken words of forgiveness or closure (that may be too late), feelings of regret, and any abuse a person has previously, or is currently experiencing.

These triggers can cause a deep sense of confusion and your loved one may or may not be able to express how they feel. This happens because they are unprepared for this particular stage of grief. This cycle of loss can feel like a curve ball, because previous hurt and trauma will continue to resurface (at the onset of any new loss) until this person has found closure and/or peace with their past hurts. As diverse as we are as individuals, the way each person processes grief is just as diverse. The more unresolved hurt your loved one has experienced in their past, the longer it will take for him or her to find healing, and gain the ability to move forward.

- Understand that your loved ones are doing their very best to make the appropriate decisions for themselves and their family, using the information they have, while in the middle of dealing with the turmoil of first-time emotions they cannot comprehend. At times, this can feel like a near-impossible task. Even decisions that seem like they should be easy to make to most people, can feel difficult and overwhelming when life is out of balance.

- Keep in mind that any unwelcomed criticism of how your loved one is handling their trial or grief will likely be perceived as a personal attack.

- Sometimes your loved one doesn't want to talk. Press once, but don't pressure. Your loved one will open up when they are ready. Consider making a note on your calendar to try again in one week.

- Unless your loved one has specifically asked you not to call, pick up the phone to see how he or she is doing. Sometimes the fear of not knowing what to say or not knowing if someone is ready to talk, can prevent many people from calling. However, one of the worst things you can do during this time of loss is to remain silent. It makes your loved one feel like they are alone and that people don't care. The family is hurting and more than ever needs to know that they are loved. If someone is not ready to receive phone calls, or if they are not ready to talk, they will allow the answering machine to pick up.

• Sometimes your loved one may not know why they are crying. It's okay to ask, but if they say, "I don't know," they probably don't know. The emotions and stages of grief can be very confusing and cause displaced emotions. Ask if he or she wants to talk through what they are feeling and if the answer is no, please be okay with that. Do your best not to press. Sometimes there are only tears and no words to express the unknown emotions faced in these moments.

• Note on your calendar any days you need to remember (commitments to follow up, birthdays, court dates, ultrasound days, doctor appointments, surgeries, cancer or illness treatment dates, anniversaries: both marriage and death, etc.). Do your best to make sure that you call your loved ones on these days; it will mean the world to them that someone remembered and is thinking of them!

Actions That Are Intentional:

o Don't just say you will pray; do it! It is so easy to get into a habit of telling people we will pray for them, simply because that is the "Christian" canned response when someone is hurting. We walk away from the situation, move on with our day and most often forget what we have committed to do. If you tell someone you will pray, write the request down where you will see it, be reminded, and then follow through. A note a day or two later, letting this person know that you prayed, will be a wonderful surprise and cause him or her to feel very loved.

o Help guide and encourage your loved one to live daily. When tragedy strikes, it can be so easy to worry and stress about things that are completely out of our control or may never come to be. Remind your loved one to look at the life of Jesus Christ as the best possible example of how to live daily.

As Jesus knelt in the Garden of Gethsemane, He prayed, *"Father, if you are willing, take this cup from me; yet not my will, but yours be done."[7]* I believe that Jesus could face his future death on the cross because months and years prior He had chosen to live daily, not consuming His mind and His heart with the tragedy of his future. Luke describes the amount of stress that Jesus endured during this prayer time with God as, *"His sweat was like drops of blood falling to the ground."[8]* However, this anguish is only mentioned on the day that Jesus knew He would be arrested, even though I imagine He knew that this moment would come long beforehand.

Jesus shows us an incredible example of *why* it is so important to live daily. How different would Jesus' ministry have been if every single day leading up to this night He experienced this same anguish and stress – concerning Himself with what would happen in the future? Jesus knew that His future was a horrific death on a cross and yet He still chose not to experience the weight of that anxiety until the time came to be. He chose to deal with His emotions on the particular day He needed to, no sooner and no later.

o If your loved one is open, submit prayer requests on their behalf with your church.

o Gather loving support around your loved one. Enlist people to pray, provide meals, provide childcare, and perform house cleaning to meet some of the daily tangible needs. Sometimes you can also anticipate other needs of the family based on your own personal experience, or the relationship you share.

o Be bold when offering to help with household chores such as laundry, paying bills, sorting mail (oh, the piles of junk mail), cleaning, washing dishes, cleaning the floors, walking or bathing the dog, mowing the lawn, changing cat litter, or taking out the trash. If you see something that needs to be done, do it. One of the best tangible things someone did for us during my last bout with cancer was not asking me, but telling me she was coming to our house to clean. She was bold and didn't give me an option. It was greatly appreciated.

o Stop talking and listen. Don't try to explain what you believe God is doing.

o Understand that it is okay to simply sit with your loved one in silence. Sometimes they just need you to be there.

o Only give advice when it is asked for.

o Let your loved ones know that you are a safe haven and open to having any conversation; that no topic or emotion is off-limits to chat about. Keep these discussions confidential, unless given permission to share, or if you believe the person is a danger to themselves or other people.

o Let your loved one also know that you are available to talk anytime, day or night, and then be available when they need you. You don't have to drop everything when they call, but understand that it is likely taking all of their strength and courage to ask for help. If it takes you days or weeks to get back to them, know that his or her courage to talk has likely dissipated by then.

o Give them a journal. It may be easier for your loved one to begin processing new information and overwhelming emotions by writing out their thoughts.

o Offer to care for their children. Take the kids out for something fun. Understand the parents may not be capable of doing this right now.

o Recognize that it's okay for your loved one to be mad at God. He is big enough to handle it! While this can be a very scary part of processing grief and dealing with difficult times, it is a normal process. Some people need to work through these emotions as they come to grips with their new circumstances. Instead of questioning his or her anger, do your best to gently create conversations to understand *why* they feel anger towards God.

o When you go to a grocery or convenience store, call and find out if there is anything you can pick up for them. Also, pick up a quick "heat and eat" meal for their family and drop it off on your way home. Ding-dong-ditch with a meal on the porch is a fantastic surprise and can make someone feel very loved. Just make sure that the family knows whom this sweet gift is from. Otherwise, it is kind of creepy!

o Call and ask if there are any errands that need to be done. Recognize your loved one may still be in the same clothes for three days straight. Sometimes going outside to do anything, changing your clothes, (or even taking a shower) requires way more energy than before.

o Understand that the pain of grief can sometimes get in the way of grieving. Provide outlets for your loved ones such as golfing or poker night for men, and a dinner or a spa day for women. Celebrate your loved one and the progress he or she has made, instead of solely focusing on their current stage of grief. Do your best to plan the night for your loved one, understanding that he or she may not be capable of making such decisions.

o Offer to set up a website where all information the grieving person wants to share can be posted in one place. It can become exhausting to share the same information and stories over and over again. There are many free websites that offer this service and can provide journaling options, as well as places for people to leave encouraging comments. If possible, maintain the website for your loved one, updating additional information as needed or desired.

o If you do not have personal experience with the trial that your loved one is facing, but know of someone who has, contact that person privately. Find out if they would be willing to talk to your loved one, or give you pointers of what he or she needed from other people when they went through their circumstances. Connect the two if and when it is appropriate.

o If you call and the person chooses not to answer the phone, please don't get frustrated. Help your loved one by not needing anything from them for a while.

o Recognize your loved one may need some time and space to process all of their emotions. If they ask you to step back for a little while, please don't be offended. They do not have the energy to feel responsible for you. Their grief is about them and they will re-engage when they are ready. That being said, don't stay away from your loved one just because you believe that all of their friends and family are already providing support. The truth is that most everyone else is thinking the same thing. Loving someone who is hurting can be such a difficult balancing act, and at times can be terribly challenging.

o Depending on how close you are, find a local support group and offer to go to a meeting with them. If this is met with resistance (which it likely will be), let him or her know that the offer stands, if and when they are ready. Leaving multiple brochures, fliers, or asking the support group to contact them will likely push your loved one away.

o Encourage your loved one to postpone any major decisions, if possible (moving, having a child, major purchases, etc.). While a clean break can be highly tempting, this is not the time for them to alter their entire lives. A good idea, however, is to encourage your loved one to go on a little getaway to begin to deal with their grief, to help them find some perspective, and to begin the process of moving forward.

o When your loved ones appear to be ready, ask how they have grown through their experiences. Attempt to guide them to focus on the positive aspects of their circumstances, instead of solely the negative.

o In some circumstances, it may be appropriate to raise money for a family to help offset medical costs or unexpected bills. There are numerous ways to spear-head this endeavor by hosting multi-family garage sales, selling personally made or baked items, hosting scrapbooking or craft parties, auctions, benefit dinners, car washes, or simply asking for donations. Many states will not allow raffles; so make sure to check with your local state law.

o Sometimes a family is grieving the death of a parent who has left behind young children. It is heartbreaking to think that these little boys and girls may be too young to remember their mom or dad as they get older. In fact, I would imagine that this is an unbearable pain to feel and process for those family members still living. Consider compiling letters from family and friends who knew the deceased to give to the children down the road. Ask people to share their favorite stories, memories, pictures, and the legacies of who their mom or dad was. This allows the life of mom or dad to carry on and gives the children a beautiful glimpse into how much mom or dad was loved, and how much mom or dad loved each one of them.

o Write down the following Bible verse and send it to your loved one in a card:

"Finally, brothers and sisters, whatever is true, whatever is noble, whatever is right, whatever is pure, whatever is lovely, whatever is admirable - if anything is excellent or praiseworthy - think about such things." –Philippians 4:8

Encourage your loved one to read this verse and break it down in the following ways when they are feeling overwhelmed with their circumstances. In regards to their trial at hand: What is true? What is noble? What is right? What is pure? What is lovely? What is admirable? What is excellent? What is praiseworthy?

Applying this verse to their present circumstances can help your loved one take their thoughts captive and prevent a spiral of overwhelming emotions. Please see Chapter Eleven for more specific details of how I personally use Philippians 4:8 when dealing with my own difficult circumstances.

o Make a list of Bible verses you would find encouraging if you were going through your loved one's trial. Send them in an email or a card.

o Understand that grief is a journey that your loved ones are unprepared to travel. Each day may be different; sometimes each hour is different. Stay consistent with them and don't build your ideas of how they are grieving based upon one conversation. If you want to be able to speak into their lives, you *must* be consistent.

o It is vitally important that you follow through and follow up with your loved one. If you commit to do something, especially after he or she has asked you for help, *please follow through*. When a person has finally gained the courage to ask for help, nothing will stop him or her from asking for help again quicker than someone failing to follow through. Check in regularly with your loved one to make sure their needs are continuing to be met, keeping in mind that their needs might change as they progress through their circumstances.

Specific Ways to Pray:

• Pray for your loved one's salvation, if he or she does not already know Jesus as his or her personal Lord and Savior. I would imagine facing any tragedy without this most important relationship would be so much more difficult and painful to endure.

- Pray that God will give the family wisdom and discernment to make difficult decisions if necessary.

- Pray through Scripture on behalf of your loved one (and perhaps, even the Bible verses you sent to him or her).

- Pray that God will draw the family close to Him and to each other during this time.

- Pray that God would bring people into their lives that can help them learn how to grieve, and process all of the new emotions they are facing.

- Pray that God will give marriages, any children, close family members, and friends, the strength they need to endure their circumstances.

- Pray that God will give parents the best words to use to help their children understand any tragic circumstances that have taken place.

- Pray for the stability and security of any children who are also suffering in this loss.

- Pray that your loved ones will feel the peace that only God can provide.

- Pray that God will meet physical and financial needs. (And, if when you are praying, He asks you to step up, step up!)

- Pray for the healing and restoration of marriages, relationships, and health.

- Pray that God will help bring calm to the chaos.

- Pray that your loved ones will be able to find rest.

- Pray that God will give your loved ones an extra dose of grace when other people make hurtful comments.

- Pray that your loved one's heart would not be hardened towards God or other people.

- Pray that your loved one will be able to make steps towards forgiving someone if that is needed.

- Pray that your loved ones will have the strength to ask for help.

- Pray for the people who surround those who are hurting to be gentle and loving.

- Pray for the Bible study times of your loved one, and that he or she will soak in the Word of God.

- Pray that God will begin to show your loved one how He can turn their awful circumstances into opportunities to come alongside other people who are hurting.

"Dear children, let us not love with words or tongue, but with actions and in truth."
—1 John 3:18

Chapter Eight

Fighting Cancer or Illness

Words That Can Be Misunderstood:

"It could have been worse!"

You are not telling your loved one anything he or she hasn't already thought of. Pointing this out only minimizes their disease. This news is still quite devastating to them.

"You can't have cancer (or illness)! You are so young!"

Unfortunately, unlike buying alcohol, there is no age limit on cancer or illness.

"You look great. You'd never know you had cancer (or illness)."

There is no scarlet letter for cancer or illness that makes each one identifiable. If you think someone looks great, let him or her know how you feel. Being encouraged in this manner will usually make your loved one smile. You don't need to end your kind words with what might be perceived as a negative connotation.

"At least you got the good kind of cancer!"

Yes, some cancers are more aggressive than others, but this disease is still devastating, even when it is likely treatable. There is no such thing as good cancer.

"You know, everything causes cancer and we are all going to get it someday. Good for you for getting yours out of the way!"

Ever since the word "cancer" stopped being taboo, people tend to believe that just about anything can cause cancer. This creates an unnecessary fear that anything touched (including a cancer patient), eaten (certain foods), walked on (treated grass), or used (cell phones) will cause one to get cancer. Cancer is awful, but don't live in a bubble of fear, especially around your loved one.

"How come you are putting on weight? I thought people with cancer lost weight?"

Once the cancer has been staged and just before treatment begins, many doctors recommend that their patients gain as much weight as possible. The additional weight can help offset the rapid weight loss during treatment when your loved one is likely unable to eat well due to fatigue, pain, or nausea.

"Oh, I think my uncle had that. He died and was in a lot of pain!"

It turned out her uncle had testicular cancer. Keep in mind, the word *cancer* is not generic or a catch all phrase for every type of cancer known to man. People diagnosed with cancer don't generally want to hear about how much pain your uncle's friend's daughter's next door neighbor's child-hood best friend had, when they too were diagnosed with cancer.

"Well, I take care of myself, eat right and exercise; so there is no way I can catch cancer!"

Cancer is not something that can be "caught." And while there are many benefits to eating well and maintaining a healthy lifestyle, there are many different causes for cancer: genetic pre-disposition, environmental factors, infections, and certain types of bacteria, to name a few. Even radiation treatment given to treat cancer can cause a different type of cancer in the future.[9] There are many athletes who care for their bodies and lead healthy lifestyles that have also been diagnosed with this devastating disease. Cancer is not biased.

"Why are you always so tired? All you want to do is sleep and you aren't fun to hang out with anymore!"

Your loved one is emotionally, physically, mentally, and sometimes spiritually exhausted. Along with the numerous doctor visits, procedures, blood tests, biopsies, and the surgeries he or she has already gone through, (in addition to potentially working or caring for their children) your loved one might also need some kind of treatment.

Gearing up for treatment takes a lot of mental toughness and emotional stability. Not only does your loved one need to choose the right treatment plan, but he or she will likely either need to allow some kind of poison to drip into his or her veins, or, they will need to lie completely immobilized on a radiation table. Neither option is the least bit desirable, and both make you feel ill.

Cancer therapy is toxic and causes many difficult-to-deal-with side effects. While some courses of treatment last a few weeks, others can last for many months. If your loved one is exhausted, let him or her sleep. They have every right to relax when they can. It is not their responsibility to entertain you while they are fighting for their life. They will need every ounce of energy they can muster, so they can heal emotionally and physically.

"Don't you wish you were a man? Men can pull off the bald look better than a woman!"

Looking back, this comment is rather funny. However, timing is everything! Don't use a comment like this while a woman is working through self-image issues and about to begin treatment. A woman undergoing chemotherapy does not wish to be a man. All she really wants is for her cancer to be effectively treated.

"Well, if you lose your hair, you know it will grow back!"

Yes, your loved one does know that eventually, someday, down the road, his or her hair will probably grow back. But hair loss is devastating and will leave your loved one feeling incredibly vulnerable.

"How come your hair hasn't fallen out? I thought you were going through cancer treatment!"

While hair loss is one of the most noticeable side effects of cancer therapy, not all treatments cause your hair to fall out.

"Is that your real hair?"

It is amazing, when you go through cancer treatments people are always so concerned about your hair. Is it real? Is it a wig? How can one tell? Enough about his or her hair; find out how the person is doing.

"You got all of that stuff for free? You are so lucky!"

There are many organizations that care for cancer patients or those with chronic illnesses, and their immediate families. But, even those families who have received the greatest donations would give everything back in a heartbeat to make their loved one cancer free.

During the staging of my first relapse, my doctor said to me, "At least you don't have kids yet to worry about!"

Having gone through cancer treatment twice without children and once with children, yes, the emotions are very different. However, there are also different sets of fears you face when you don't already have children.

Fears like: "If I have chemo, will I become sterile?" or "If I am able to get pregnant, will I be able to give birth to a healthy child?" These thoughts are scary for a lot of women who might not only be making life and death decisions for her own health, but who are having to weigh out the future consequences of the choices she makes for her treatment plan.

Since many women place their personal worth and value in relationships, choosing a treatment option can be a devastating decision on many different levels. Your loved one may struggle with grieving the loss of children and a family she doesn't know if she will ever be able to have. And, she may or may not be comfortable sharing these emotions with those closest to her for fear that others will dismiss her feelings, or simply tell her not to worry about it. Her emotions are normal, yet often times will go unnoticed by doctors, families, and friends.

"What in the world will you do if your cancer (or illness) ever comes back? Doesn't that completely terrify you?"

Of course the thought of a cancer or other illness relapse can be scary! However, if this happens, your loved one will do the same thing he or she did the first time. They will put one foot in front of the other and deal with his or her new circumstances one day at a time.

Living in fear of an illness relapse causes undue stress and will limit the joy your loved one can feel conquering or managing their disease. Enjoy life with your loved one, instead of focusing on what may or may not happen in the future. Tomorrow is never promised. Live today!

"What is your life expectancy?" or "How long have the doctors given you?"

None of us know the day or hour we will die (and I think that is a good thing). The life expectancy of a cancer patient or someone living with a chronic illness is to become cancer free, or to find and maintain a balance with their disease, not to die.

Avoid any comments beginning with the statement, "I'm sure you don't want to hear this, but..."

Unless you are a doctor giving bad news, if you are already questioning the delivery of your statement, please reconsider if what you want to say really needs to be said.

Words That Encourage:

"How is your spouse doing? What can we do for him/her?"

Often times, others can overlook a spouse in the midst of a cancer or illness diagnosis. A spouse believes his or her role is to be strong, steady, and unwavering. But, the reality is he or she feels terrified of losing their beloved and will have to conquer their own set of fears. They may grieve this disease in a very different way.

"How are your children doing? What can we do for them?"

Children also tend to get overlooked during trials of newly diagnosed diseases. Some children may be too young to understand what is going on, but can definitely feel the stressful environment and change. Offering play dates, outings, childcare, and fun activities will give both the parents and the children a much-needed break. If your loved one has a couple of weeks before treatment or therapy begins, start play dates early to help promote stability, so everything is not changing at the exact same time.

"You are beautiful!" or "You are handsome!"

For the most part, our world only views beauty on the outside. People who have cancer don't always (if rarely ever) feel beautiful or attractive. Not only is there the potential for rapid weight loss during treatment, but also if your loved one loses his or her hair, he or she will likely feel vulnerable and unattractive. There are few men or women that can rock the bald look with confidence from the first time they see a pile of hair left behind on their pillows. Let people struggling through cancer treatment know that you think they look amazing. Your words may be received with eyes rolled and a self-demeaning response, but deep down in their hearts, you have just made their day!

"I imagine you might be afraid of what people will think when you tell them you have cancer (or another illness). Well, I think you are incredible and amazing!"

"I cannot imagine how difficult learning about this diagnosis must have been for you. What can I do to ease some of your fears?"

"I cannot believe you are going through this. Please talk to me about how you are feeling."

"This cancer (or illness) does not define you!"

"Talk to me about what happened at your appointment/treatment."

"Besides the cancer (or illness), what else is on your mind?"

This is so important! Talk about something other than their cancer, illness, doctor appointments, therapy drugs, and treatments. Most of a cancer patient's life or the life of someone struggling through illness revolve around doctor's visits, tests, treatment, and a whole lot of confusing information. What a great reprieve to be able to talk about something else.

"What can I bring to make your hospital stay a little bit more comfortable for you?"

"You are one of the strongest people I know!"

"I will not pretend that I can come close to understanding what you are going through, but please talk to me about how you are feeling!"

Your loved one doesn't need you to understand. He or she just needs you to be there!

"I admire the way you are handling your circumstances!"

"You are such an inspiration to me!"

A few more things to remember:

• Understand that one of the greatest obstacles for your loved one to face and overcome is the fear of the unknown. At times this fear can become crippling and difficult to manage. This is another reason why it is good to remind your loved one to live daily. Trying to live in the future can be very overwhelming because there are endless potential outcomes.

• Keep up to date on your immunizations and flu shots. Staying healthy while caring for someone with a compromised immune system is very important.

• Do your best not to treat a cancer patient, someone with a chronic illness, or a cancer survivor like they are diseased or handicapped.

• Understand that a headache is no longer just a headache to a cancer patient; in their mind, it is a tumor. A tumor, they believe whole-heartedly will cause a brain aneurysm, that will burst and cause them to stroke out. They are scared that this "tumor" will elongate treatment, take them out of remission, or kill them.

    The same goes with a stomachache, a sore throat, any swollen lymph node, a backache, leg pain, gas pains, indigestion, a hangnail, or an ingrown hair. Seriously. I had a hang nail on my toe that caused a lymph node to swell up in my groin and my first reaction was to believe I had two months left to live. In time, these fears will subside and eventually pass, but they can be very real to a cancer patient. Do your best to gently talk your loved one down and try to understand their frame of mind. Thinking clearly and logically can be very different after someone has been diagnosed with a potential life-threatening disease they cannot control.

- Recognize that life doesn't always just go on after cancer treatment. More often than not, your loved one cannot pick up right where they left off before they received their diagnosis. Their entire worldview and sometimes their faith, has been completely shaken and altered.

   After the proactive portion of killing the cancer is gone, there are still some volatile emotions to deal with. This person has just looked death square in the face. Keep in mind that post-treatment depression is a very real possibility, but that this depression may also be delayed a month or two once your loved one has come off of the high of being done with treatments and beginning remission. That being said, your loved one can still fall back in love with life after fighting cancer. In fact, your loved one can live a life with a greater, more clearly defined purpose after fighting cancer. The best way to set him or her up for success is to remain consistent and loving.

- Refrain from talking with your loved one about cancer or illness horror stories or focusing on harrowing survival rates.

Actions That Are Intentional:

o Understand if people choose not to share their cancer or illness diagnosis with you right away. They are likely trying to wrap their brain around the devastating news of their disease. Please do not take it personally. They are not intending to hurt you. In fact, they are likely trying to figure out how to inform you of their difficult circumstances without causing you pain.

o If possible, research your loved one's cancer or illness just a little bit on a trusted medical site like WebMd® so that you have a baseline of understanding. Many people have been asked to share the history of their cancer or illness countless times to numerous people and this can be very exhausting.

o Offer to go to doctor's appointments or treatments with your loved one. Waiting in the reception area alone feels lonely. This act of kindness will speak volumes.

o Offer rides to and from the hospital, especially during cancer treatments. There will be many times when your loved one will be too tired to function properly and should not be driving a vehicle. Benadryl is often given with many chemotherapy drugs to help minimize side effects and allergic reactions. This will make your loved one very drowsy and unsafe on the road. Approach him or her with this idea in a manner that relays that you want to spend time with your loved one, instead of pointing out all of the reasons why he or she should not be driving. Doing the latter, will only cause your loved one to want to prove you wrong.

o Consider giving your loved one a notepad or journal. Encourage him or her to start a list of all the things that happen throughout the week that encourage him or her. This can help your loved one focus on the positive aspects of what is happening around him or her, instead of being weighed down by negativity.

o Create a fun, three-ring notebook for your loved one where they can begin to keep copies of their medical records. This has been absolutely vital for me to not only have all of my records in one place, but to not have to wait for busy doctors (with many other patients) to fax over medical records when needed. Sometimes based on a person's medical history, there will be a doctor who will start connecting the dots and might need medical records your loved one did not think to ask a previous doctor to send. Encourage your loved one to also keep copies of all radiology scans. (Radiology Departments will make them a copy if they ask before the procedures.) Consider placing dividers in the notebook, so that your loved one can easily flip to the information they need. For instance, I currently use the following dividers and system which has worked very well for me:

1. Ruled paper where I can jot down notes or any questions I have for my doctor
2. CBC's – Complete Blood Counts
3. Other blood work, organized by date (I break this down with additional dividers for specific tests that I know my doctors are tracking.)
4. Surgical Procedure Reports
5. Non-Surgical Procedure Reports
6. Biopsy Reports
7. Scan Reports (CT, MRI, PET, EKG, Echo's, etc.)
8. Treatment Reports
9. Doctors Information (If you can find plastic business card inserts for three-ring binders, these work perfectly.)

o Keep in mind that a few days before cancer treatments begin, your loved one will likely be very emotional, feel unprepared, and question everything. Questions will pop up seemingly out of nowhere like, "Am I making the right decision about treatment?" "Will this treatment be effective?" "What if the cancer doesn't kill me, but the chemo does?"

This is a normal process for cancer patients and typically (based on my research) lasts 24–36 hours. Do not be surprised if your normally peace-filled loved one becomes overwhelmed by the fear of the unknown. There are many chemotherapy drugs that have caused death during the very first infusion. Two days before my first chemotherapy treatment, I wrote goodbye letters to my husband and children. The fear of the unknown and potentially leaving them behind were very real enemies I needed to face and conquer.

o If hospitalized for surgery, illness, or treatment, ask your loved one if they have any special requests for food or drinks, if permitted. Hospital food gets old very quickly.

o Pick up a special book, journal, activity, or create a care package for your loved one. Bring it to the hospital the day treatment begins or during a long stay for an illness. I still smile when I see or use some of the items brought for me during these times. To this day, I still have something special that my volleyball teammates gave me from 1999!

o Pick up or create a skin care basket for your loved one undergoing chemotherapy. Many drugs used will make his or her skin itchy and dry. Include items like, special lotions for dry skin, oatmeal bath packs, hypo-allergenic items, moisturizing socks and gloves, bath oils (stay away from salts that may further irritate the skin), exfoliating scrubs, and for men, a toy boat destroyer to make it a "man bath."

o Understand that undergoing treatment for cancer or illnesses can make a person very irritable. Show as much grace as possible during these weeks and months, and try your best not to let your feelings get hurt easily.

o Also understand that as most treatments progress, the side effects get exponentially worse. Enlist as much help as possible during the last couple of treatments. Your loved one will likely be feeling emotionally and physically depleted and may not know what he or she needs.

o If you are the primary caregiver to your loved one, allow yourself at least a weekly break. Doing this is not selfish! Caring for someone through cancer or illness is tough and emotionally, physically, and spiritually draining. You need to take care of yourself, so that you can take care of your loved one.

o If you are not the primary caregiver, offer to step into that role for a day to give that person a break. Their role is exhausting and this reprieve is very much needed, whether they ask for it or not. If they resist you, press gently, but don't push!

o If you are gutsy and your loved one loses their hair during treatment, shave your head and surprise them. Or ladies, if you have ten inches of hair to cut off, consider donating it to Locks of Love.[10] This will mean so much to your loved one, while reminding you to pray for him or her every time you see your new hairdo. In 1999, some of my volleyball teammates decided they were going to shave their heads if I had to undergo chemotherapy and lost my hair. There is no doubt in my mind that some of them would have done it in a heartbeat. However, there was definitely a hint of relief when I told the ladies that I only needed radiation therapy!

o Focus on life, not death.

o Plan a small vacation or weekend getaway for a few months after treatment is over, or even in the middle of treatment, if your loved one is up for it. Give them something to look forward to, plan for, and dream about.

o Know that it is okay to laugh. Find DVD's or audio soundtracks of Christian comedians to listen to together. Sometimes laughter can help release some of the pent up emotional energy in a positive way. Grab some snacks and create a fun night with your loved one. Some of these great men and women can speak a lot of truth through their humor.[11]

o Write down "Remission Month" on your calendar after your loved one has gone through cancer treatment and has a clean bill of health. Each year, during that month, celebrate that victory.

This is a big deal for cancer survivors and goes unnoticed by most people.

o Hug your loved one and tell them you love them. Many people are afraid to touch someone with cancer or an illness because they think they can catch it.

Specific Ways to Pray:

- Pray for your loved one's salvation, if he or she does not already know Jesus as his or her personal Lord and Savior. Facing death can be scary, even for those who know that their eternity is secure in Heaven. Imagine how much more scary it can be, if you don't know what will happen to you after you die.

- Pray that God will give the family wisdom and discernment to make the difficult decisions of whether or not to undergo surgeries, to figure out what medical tests and procedures to perform, and to decide how to proceed with cancer or illness treatments.

- Pray that God would bring your loved one another cancer or chronic illness survivor with a similar journey (and age if possible) that can help your loved one learn how to navigate the new world of medical doctors, facilities, terminology, insurance, and all of the first-time emotions of processing a new illness.

- Pray for the spouse or significant other of the one who has recently been diagnosed with cancer or another illness. Pray that God will bring a sense of calm when needed, boldness and courage when needed, strength and resolve when needed, and to provide respite and rest when needed.

- Pray that God will give your loved ones the words to use to talk with their children about the diagnosis in a non-scary, optimistic way. Pray that God will give them strength of emotion when discussing why dad or mom needs to go to the hospital so much, why he or she might be losing his or her hair, and what the near future might hold.

- Pray that God will give the doctors wisdom and discernment to understand what is going on, and how to effectively treat the cancer or illness. Also pray that the doctors will be proactive in the care of your loved one and gentle when giving out difficult to hear information.

- Pray that God will meet physical and financial needs. For many people, every medical bill serves as a reminder of the devastation of their disease and may place your loved one in a challenging situation where they may or may not choose treatment, or additional diagnostic tests based on whether or not they feel they can afford to pay for them.

- Pray for the strength of your loved one to endure the toll of chemotherapy or radiation treatments.

- Pray for healing. Our God is a big God!

- Pray for your loved one's sense of self-worth. With certain cancers, body parts may need to be removed in order to aid in the success rate of bringing a person successfully into remission. If this happens with your loved one, he or she may feel like less of a man or woman. He or she may grieve these losses.

- Pray for clarity of thought for your loved one and the ability to ask the right questions at doctor's appointments and during the decision-making processes of how to move forward. These appointments can be so overwhelming.

- Pray for the health and wellness of other family members. Any sign of sickness, a cold, a virus, or a bacterial infection, can have devastating effects on someone with a compromised immune system.

"Suppose a brother or sister is without clothes, and daily food. If one of you says to them, 'Go, I wish you well; keep warm and well fed,' but does nothing about his physical needs, what good is it? In the same way, faith by itself, if it is not accompanied by action, is dead."
—James 2:15–17

Chapter Nine

Grieving the Loss of a Child

Words That Can Be Misunderstood:

Miscarriage

"This was for the best. There was probably something wrong with your baby anyway."

The fact that there was likely something wrong with their child is what is completely breaking their heart. Your loved one is questioning everything she ate, how much she did or didn't sleep, how much exercise she did or didn't get, while wondering what she did wrong, or what she could have done differently. These kinds of words only cause your loved ones to blame themselves more and feel responsible for their child's death.

"Since I didn't see you pregnant, it's like your child never existed (or, this never happened)."

Few other comments will shut down communication and cause conflict in a relationship quicker than this type of comment. Many women miscarry before a pregnant belly tells the world what beautiful gift is growing within them. Other times, a person may go through an entire pregnancy where family and friends may never see the pregnancy due to geographical location—that doesn't make their child or the hopes and dreams they had for him or her any less real just because the evidence wasn't seen.

"Your baby was only a fetus. He/She wasn't real."

Every part of their child was real—he or she had a soul, a head, a heart, arms, and legs. Babies can taste, blink their eyes, kick their legs, and get hiccups in utero. This family's child was a tiny human being growing and living within his or her mother.[12]

"This miscarriage could be a blessing in disguise!"

The pain and agony caused by a miscarriage is not a blessing.

"At least you know you can get pregnant!"

This is not helpful. The word "infertility" does not only encompass those people who cannot get pregnant. It is also a term for women who can get pregnant, but cannot carry a child to term. Whether a person is unable to conceive, or is able to conceive and not bring a child into the world, the family is still completely devastated.

"You can always have another child."

Their child was never disposable and will never be replaced, regardless if they choose to have more children. There is also a possibility there may be biological issues that will not allow them to carry a child to term. These are discussions to be had between the couple and their doctor.

"I hope you take this as a sign that you shouldn't have any more babies!"

While there could be a lot of truth to this statement when a woman has undergone multiple miscarriages, hearing these words are rarely ever taken in the way they are intended. Instead, engage in a conversation about this topic by asking what your loved one is thinking about future pregnancies. She may very well believe having more children is out of the question, but allowing her to say this (instead of you), prevents her from becoming defensive and opens up the lines of communication.

"It's not your fault."

This will need to be said, but with great caution, at the right time, and by the right person. Keep this saying to yourself, unless you are a spouse, a best friend, or a parent, and then proceed with great caution. Your loved one feels responsible for the death of her child. She believes she failed. She feels inadequate as a wife (she couldn't give her husband a child) and inadequate as a mother (possibly believing that she killed her own child). Your loved one feels like she should have protected her child from harm and while normal, this stage of grief is complicated to process.

"You can always adopt!"

While adoption can be beautiful, it is not a last resort for people who are unable to conceive or carry children naturally. A comment like this one suggests to your loved one that he or she is inadequate to biologically produce a child. Hearing these words will often times put your loved one in a defensive position, while creating a desire within him or her to prove you wrong!

Men and women struggling with infertility want to choose an alternative to biologically producing a child on their own terms, nobody else's. This is a very difficult part of the grieving process to accept and find peace with. If you want to create conversations with your loved ones about the possibility of adoption, ask questions and do your best to refrain from using statements. For instance, "I know that adoption may not be right for your family, but is it something you've thought about?"

"How many more babies are you going to kill?"

As appalling as this statement is, I was completely shocked to learn how common it is for those who suffer miscarriages to hear someone say these words. A woman who has miscarried already feels responsible for the death of her child. A comment like this only causes her to continue blaming herself, instead of progressing through her journey to understand that the miscarriage was not her fault!

Infant or Child Death and Failed Adoptions

"It must have been God's will." or "This was just part of God's plan."

Even if you are very close, unless your loved ones are specifically seeking your spiritual counseling, steer away from any comments suggesting that the death of their child or a failed adoption was God's intention for their family. For a grieving person hearing these words, it is easy to feel like, "If this is God's plan, then I want nothing to do with God!"

"At least your child didn't live long enough for you to really get attached!" Or, "At least the adoption failed before you really got attached!"

Personally speaking, every single moment my daughter Kylie was growing within me, I was getting attached. She was real from the moment I found out about her, the days I spent feeling nauseated, and every time I felt her precious kicks. I was so attached to her that I had made the decision to give my life for her if I needed to.

Likewise, from the moment we began our adoption journey, I was growing an attachment to the child that would one day be our son or daughter. As soon as we were "matched" with the first birth mother, we began our emotional attachment to JT. The attachment a family has for their biological child or a potential-adoptive child, is not based on how many minutes, hours, or days that child lived, or was in their care. Their attachment is based on the depth of their love for that son or daughter.

"He just wasn't your baby!"

This was said by quite a few people regarding our failed adoption and was very painful to hear. Everything inside my husband and I felt *that* little boy was meant to be our son. Only God (not JT's mother, or even our family) knows whether God's best was chosen for him. As humans, we constantly prove that we don't always choose, or sometimes accept, God's best.

"Be grateful for the children you have."

Not only are your loved ones so incredibly grateful for the children they can still hold in their arms, but they are terrified something bad will happen to them as well.

"You should really hold your friend's baby so that you can prove to them how much you love them!"

It will take all of the courage and strength your friend can muster to be around another baby, let alone hold another child for a long time. Your friend has nothing to prove to you or to anyone else. Expecting her to do this before she is ready will only cause undue pressure and resentment. Your loved one will hold another child when she is ready. Dear reader, *she will get there*, but it needs to be on her terms and nobody else's.

This moment for me happened about five months after Kylie died as I fed our friends' baby. It was just the two of us and I cried nearly uncontrollably. I was so grateful (and relieved) to not be around other people while I came to grips with these emotions. All I could think about was how much I wanted to feed my own child and how desperately I wanted to hold her again.

These feelings slowly gave way to a unique acceptance and closure to Kylie's death that I had not yet experienced. Had other people been around, I likely would not have gotten to this place. This moment was powerful, emotional, and led to a deeper healing. It enabled me to begin to move forward from Kylie's death, which was very much needed. However, holding another baby needed to happen at the right place, the right time, and for me, with the right family.

"Your child is in a better place."

Yes, Heaven is absolutely better than anything this world can offer, but what your loved one most desires right now is to hold his or her child. There is a missing piece in their family now, a void that cannot be replaced. The baby's bedroom is vacant, his or her crib is empty. There are clothes and toys that may never be worn or played with. There may be siblings constantly questioning why their brother or sister is gone. The couple knows they could have provided an incredible amount of love, support, and every opportunity for their child to chase their wildest dreams.

"Now you have an angel watching over you."

The Bible never tells us that people turn into angels when they go to Heaven. Rather the Bible shares that God specifically created angels separately from when He created humans. When dealing with child loss, many people really don't want to think of their child as an angel.

"Time heals all wounds!"

This is another empty platitude. While time helps ease the intensity of their pain, complete healing will only happen when God restores all brokenness in Heaven.

"It's almost been a year. You really need to get over it."

Coming upon the first year anniversary of the death of a child and sometimes a failed adoption can be very overwhelming and intense. These dates are an enormous milestone for parents to overcome. The volatile emotions of anticipating this date for many families begin about six weeks prior to the anniversary. What happened will be an integral part of this couple and their family, for the rest of their lives. They will never be the same again. Don't pressure them to move on or tell them they are grieving too long. This will actually slow their healing. Their grief will ease on its own timeline, not yours.

"You have no idea of the hell you put my pregnant wife through when your baby died!"

This is quite possibly one of the most offensive, selfish, and shocking statements someone said to us. We felt personally attacked through circumstances we could not control. It is great to let people know that you are grieving with and for them—to show that the death of a child did not go unnoticed. But, please don't make the death of their child about you and how your family processed their devastating news.

<u>Words That Encourage:</u>

"I can't imagine the pain you felt when your daughter/son died."

Yes, specifically use the word "died" and remember to use the name of your loved one's child. Acknowledge their pain, even when it is uncomfortable for you. This will show that you are open to talking about how your loved one truly feels. A comment like this will potentially also open up the doors for him or her to start talking about their emotions and hurt with you. But, please, let it be on his or her terms. Don't force the conversation.

"Your child is so loved!"

"How is your husband (or wife) doing? What can we do for him (or her)?"

"You are in our thoughts and prayers!"

"We are praying that you and your spouse will cling to each other through this trial and that God will give you the peace that only He can provide!"

"Your child has touched the lives of so many people!"

"Your child was unique and irreplaceable. The fact that you have another child does not lessen the grief of losing this one."

If you have experienced the death of a child: "Dealing with the loss of a child is one of the most difficult trials you will ever go through. Please don't feel like you need to do this alone!"

"Words cannot express how much my heart breaks for what you are going through! What can I do?"

"Thank you for trusting me with your story (or feelings). I cannot imagine that was easy for you."

"I know there is nothing I can say to make this better, but please know that I will commit to pray for you and your family."

"I am available if you need someone to talk to."

"I'm going to call you next week, just to check on you." (Then, please make sure you do!)

"Grief is unpredictable. There is no right or wrong way to go through it."

"Don't feel guilty because you laughed today. It's okay!"

"Talk to me about your little girl/boy!"

"What are your favorite memories of your child?"

"Please talk about your feelings and memories of your baby. I know you haven't forgotten about your child just because I'm afraid to talk about him/her."

As often as you can remember, use the name of your loved one's child when you offer your condolences, discuss the events that took place, or create conversations. While this may feel uncomfortable, it shows that you value the child that has died and their grief. In addition, many families will love to hear others speak the name of their child who has died.

When asked, "How do I deal with this pain?" respond with, "One day at a time! Sometimes, one hour at a time!"

"There is no timetable for you to work through the emotions of your child's death. Work them out in your own time and know that I am available whenever you need me."

A few more things to remember:

- Do your best to stay away from comparing any miscarriage, child death, or failed adoption you have also experienced, along with any other difficult trial you may have faced in your life. There is no need to get into discussions of who may have had a more difficult event in life, or grieving process.

- Men, if you can get over the awkwardness of what I am about to say, here is a little nugget for you. Your wife or significant other will likely feel a pendulum swing of emotions right after the death of your child via miscarriage. One week, she may tell you that she never wants to have children again, and is requesting you to make an appointment with your doctor to take permanent measures. One week later, you may find that she is unable to get pregnancies out of her brain and all she wants is another baby *right now!* This will leave you confused and likely questioning her sanity. (Don't worry; she is questioning her sanity too!)

   Yet, in God's perfect design, He has created your beautiful woman's body to do exactly what it should during her ovulation cycles. Hormones are raging and the emotions she feels are very difficult to understand. Her body is telling her one thing; while her heart and mind likely another.

   Though she may not realize what is happening, in reality, it may not be another baby she wants. She might just miss the baby she has lost and desperately wants to finish out her pregnancy with *that* child. Do your best to remain steadfast and guide discussions to decide as a couple, *during non-ovulation times,* the minimum time frame you would like to wait before trying to conceive once again. Most OB/GYNs will recommend at least three months.[13] Personally, I needed a lot longer.

- When a miscarriage is the very first pregnancy experience of your loved one, expect that she will fear even the *possibility* of any future pregnancies. Your loved one may temporarily grieve a family she doesn't know whether or not she will be able to have. This may cause her to want to hurry up and try to get pregnant again in order to prove to herself that she (and her body) can do it. Understand that this miscarriage is her baseline and to this point, is all she knows.

- Understand that going back to church can be emotionally exhausting for a woman and will likely take weeks from the death of her child to build up the courage to do so. Coming face to face with so many men and women in the same place who knew that she was pregnant, or that the child died, is very overwhelming.

     My first day back to church after Kylie died was heartbreaking for me. I spent most of the singing portion of the worship service crying, with every song somehow reminding me of my little girl. I was then met with the awkwardness of some people not knowing that Kylie had died and asking how our pregnancy was going. We then went to our Bible Study where nobody really knew how to react or respond, us included. While going back to church was an important step for us to get back into a routine, it was emotionally and physically exhausting.

- Please don't judge your loved one because they are not acting the way you believe they should, especially if you have never experienced the death or loss of a child. If your loved one is vulnerable enough to share feelings of jealousy over someone else's pregnancy, or struggling to be happy with the safe arrival of a friend's child, understand these are normal feelings and a part of her process of grief.

- Sometimes there are feelings and emotions that just don't have any names.

- If you are currently pregnant, please do not share how much you are dreading your pregnancy, complain about every symptom you have, or talk about how you can't wait for your pregnancy to be over. Your loved one would give just about anything to be in your shoes.

- If you find yourself in an unplanned or unexpected pregnancy, under no circumstances share that you are hoping you miscarry your child to a woman who has experienced this pain. Also, please do not talk about how much you wish you were not pregnant. Comments like these will completely devastate your loved one and will likely cause feelings of bitterness and resentment. If you are unprepared to care for your child, there are many families that will lovingly adopt your baby and treat him or her as their own.

- While I believe a distorted reality can happen with any kind of trial, for me, this was never truer than dealing with the death of Kylie. Not only did I blame myself for her death; at one point, as I mentioned earlier, I believed that I killed her. While I was the only one living in this distorted reality, for a very long time nobody could talk me out of it!

  When my husband, family or friends would tell me that Kylie's death was not my fault, it wasn't that I didn't believe them, I simply did not agree with them. To me, it was a difference of opinion. It wasn't a right or wrong issue. It was a right or left issue. Instead of soaking in that Kylie's death was not my fault (and that I did not kill her), I would defend and attempt to point out every reason why her death was in fact, my fault.

  I questioned every decision I made of not intervening on her behalf, especially because she lived for eighty minutes. I also believed my body failed her. I could not comprehend how I was not responsible for her death. The people closest to me, in many ways, had to sit back and allow me to process "fact" vs. "my fiction".

  It took me a very long time to truly accept that Kylie's death was not my fault, to stand up to Satan attacking my weakness, and to forgive myself of the blame. What a difficult and dark road traveled, but what mercy, grace, love, and freedom was gained when I could finally let go and accept the reality that everyone else could clearly see!

- There may come a point in your loved one's journey when they find themselves struggling through extreme jealousy and will possibly become very judgmental. While not always right, these are normal cycles of dealing with grief. Your loved one may feel tempted to be the parent police, criticizing the parental skills (or sometimes lack thereof) of those they see around them. They may struggle with feelings like, "Why do *they* get a bunch of children, but I don't?"

  I once had the raging desire to tell off a stranger for screaming at her very young children in what I deemed was a completely inappropriate manner. In fact, I had to walk out of the store because I was beginning to lose all semblance of control. I was literally shaking I was so angry. These types of emotions can become constant struggles if not appropriately dealt with.

  Do your best to be gentle when this happens. Let your loved one vent and once they have calmed down, go back to him or her and talk through how they felt. If you attempt to correct their behavior in the heat of the moment, their frustrations may get turned on you and you may lose the opportunity to get to the heart of their pain.

- Understand that a failed adoption is very similar to the death of a biologically born child. Your loved ones will struggle through the death of this relationship and will grieve every hope and dream they had for that child. In many different ways, our failed adoption was much more difficult to deal with than the death of our biological daughter, or our miscarriages.

- Consider a completed adoption right after a failed adoption as you would a miscarriage.

  If a couple miscarries and becomes pregnant a few weeks or months later, resulting in the healthy delivery of another child, the couple is faced with an unusual perspective. As much as they love, cherish, and adore their newborn baby, the couple would not be holding that particular child had they not experienced the death of their previous one.

  Had the couple carried their first child to delivery, they would never have known about the child they now hold in their arms. In fact, this newborn baby would not even exist. However, the exact feelings they have for their newborn child are the same feelings they would have had for their first child, had that child not died.

In the same way, had we not experienced our failed adoption, we would never have known about our now-adopted son. To our family, it would have been like he never existed. We would have loved, cherished, and adored JT, with the same emotions we now have for our son. While we cannot imagine life without our incredible little boy (and we truly wouldn't have it any other way), we are still faced with a unique perspective having him as a part of our family.

- Remember the death of a child is the absolute worst tragedy your loved ones have likely experienced. Please don't share stories of the death of your dog or cat and state that you know what the family is going through. While I understand many pets are "like family" to different people, these types of comments are very devastating for your loved ones to hear.

- Please don't compare the grief you feel over choosing an abortion to the pain your loved ones feel burying their child. It is not the same.

- If your loved one chooses to get pregnant again, please keep in mind what their family has been through. The new pregnancy, while exciting, is also completely terrifying. Out of fear of dealing with another broken heart, a woman may distance herself emotionally from the child she carries for a period of time. She may struggle through the fear of the unknown and constantly question whether or not this child will also meet an early death. This is her defense and coping mechanism.

Expect there will be a negative transfer of emotions, especially in the first trimester. For women who have miscarried, many will live in fear of the pregnancy from the minute she finds out she is pregnant, until after her child is born. If a family has experienced the death of a child due to SIDS, or after-birth complications, a woman is likely to live in fear from the time she learns of her new pregnancy until she passes the length of time when her other child died (if not longer). While normal, these are very difficult emotions to work through and process. Encourage your loved one to bring her fears before God and pray specifically for these emotions.

Actions That Are Intentional:

o Recognize that men grieve the deaths of their children too, but their grief may be delayed. In our circumstances, it was six months before my husband began his journey to grieve the death of our daughter Kylie. He was so concerned about making sure that I was okay, that without either one of us realizing it, he postponed dealing with his own emotions.

o Keep in mind that men also compartmentalize their problems and may have a challenging time admitting that they are hurting for fear of showing weakness. Just because a man is doing well (or even excelling) in his job, it does not mean the traumatic experiences he has faced are over, that he is done grieving (or has even started), or that his family doesn't still need help. When my husband was unable to control my cancer, the death of our daughter, or our failed adoption, it was very easy for him to feel like he could control his work and his career. Sometimes a man's work can become consuming because the stress at home feels (is) so out of control.

o Siblings will also grieve the loss of a brother or sister and may or may not be able to put their grief into words. If you consider how challenging it can be for adults to express their feelings, imagine how difficult it might be for a child. Arrange a play date and allow the children to ask any questions they might have. Shortly after our failed adoption, our daughter was so devastated and confused, that anytime Todd would go to work, she believed he was not coming home. This was another reason for our grief vacation, to provide some stability for her to know that Todd was not going anywhere and would always come home from work, as his military schedule would allow.

o Offer to help with funeral arrangements. This can be extremely overwhelming.

o Offer to set up a memorial fund for their child. Find out what organizations are important to the family and instead of sending flowers, donate on behalf of their child. Encourage others to do the same. We asked people to consider donating to March of Dimes® or Focus on the Family® after our daughter died. When people did this, we were sent e-mails or cards from the organizations letting us know that someone had donated on behalf of our little girl. This was absolutely precious to us and I still have the cards to this day.

o Purchase a nice gift of remembrance for the family. We had friends give us a beautiful memory box that we were able to engrave, another friend made us a memory box, and my parents gave me a beautiful locket. I actually keep a copy of Kylie's footprints in that locket. These gifts are still precious to our family.

   The year Kylie died, we had two other friends experience the death of their children as well. I purchased snowflake ornaments that could be engraved and sent them to our friends as a Christmas gift (and I kept one for our family too). Every year, as we put up our Christmas tree, I am not only able to keep Kylie close, but I am reminded to pray for our dear friends who are also celebrating another holiday season without their sweet children.

o Offer to go with your loved one to her follow up OB/GYN appointment after a miscarriage, pre-term delivery, or infant loss. This is a very difficult, but important milestone. Walking back into the doctor's office no longer pregnant takes a tremendous amount of courage and may be met with a lot of resistance. Bring tissues and maybe even some chocolate! Knowing the likelihood your loved one will come face-to-face with another woman sporting a beautiful, big pregnant belly is tremendously difficult.

o Once the family has decided what to do with their child's belongings, offer to help them sort through toys, clothes, and furniture. If their intention is to donate these items, offer to take the belongings to the donation center for them. This prevents the additional stress and emotion of driving to the donation center, wondering if your loved one will feel obligated to explain why she is crying over her donation.

o Make or buy a worship CD for your loved one. Two different people did this for us, one after Kylie's death and one after our failed adoption. It took me quite a few months to be able to listen to the CD after we had Kylie, but the worship CD given to us after we gave JT back, sustained me and kept me on my feet.

o Purchase a rose bush or a tree that your loved one can plant in their yard to commemorate their child.

o Recognize that a person is forever changed after they have buried their child or miscarried. Their views of life and death are completely altered and difficult to work through.

o Understand if you get pregnant (or are currently pregnant) when your loved one experiences the death of their child, it may be very difficult to be your friend right now. Please be as patient and understanding as you can. Even though you may be close, your loved one may not be ready to be around a pregnant woman or hear about the joys of your pregnancy. She will get there; it just may take some time.

My best friend was pregnant at the same time I was pregnant with Kylie. In fact, our due dates were just two months apart. What an awkward position she must have been in, as we were both so excited to be pregnant together. Yet, she was so sensitive to how I was feeling and right away told me that she would not bring up her pregnancy unless I asked to hear about what was going on. This was amazing and gave me the permission to ask about her pregnancy when I was ready to hear about it, without creating an awkward "elephant in the room" every time we talked.

When her son was born, I cried, and I cried, and then I cried some more. I was truly so happy for them, but so sad for us. To this day, my best friend continues to be incredible about taking into consideration how I feel when her son reaches new milestones. She even took my feelings into consideration when she found out that she had conceived a little girl, and then made sure I was okay the first time I held her daughter, who was born the day before Kylie would have been four years old.

We love and cherish both of their children as if they were our own. But, what made this possible was her ability to gently love me by giving me permission to grieve, to verbalize that I was sad about the broken dreams we had made for our children, and to give me some space when I needed it, without judgment or condemnation. What a great friend to have!

o Send a note or card. Each one received will make the family feel as though their child is cared for and loved. Please don't be angry if your loved ones don't write back or respond. Love them with no strings attached or expectation.

o Don't pretend the death of their child didn't happen and don't change the subject when they bring it up. If a man or woman is sharing their grief with you, it means they trust you. They are talking about their emotions because they want to, not because they feel like they have to. Sharing their pain and the process of their grieving takes an immense amount of courage and a lot of vulnerability. If you change the subject, they will likely stop opening up to you.

o Understand that being around women who are pregnant is very uncomfortable for a woman hurting over the loss of her child. The truth is she feels jealous, insecure, and will grieve her child all over again. Many women struggle with feelings of what could have been, and wondering what may have happened had she done something differently, instead of being grounded in the reality of what *is*. More than four years after Kylie's death, I still relapse into this mentality every once in awhile.

o   Please understand if your loved ones do not attend baby showers, baby dedications, and birthday parties. They will tiptoe into this arena when they are ready. Attempting to talk them into these activities will only cause a lot of anxiety and additional stress, stunting the progress they have already made.

o   Keep in mind there is a severe grieving process of not only the death of relationship, but also the death of all hopes and dreams the family had for this child. The most unusual circumstances will remind your loved ones of their child, when they realize they have "lost" another dream (such as a father walking his daughter down the aisle on her wedding day, never teaching his son how to play catch, a mom never seeing her little girl's excitement over meeting a Disney Princess, or seeing her son's face light up by racecars or monster trucks, etc.). These broken dreams can come up unexpectedly and most often, the couple is completely un-prepared to deal with them.

o   Realize that a woman may experience a time of complete over-protectiveness. This is a normal part of her grieving process and emotions that are difficult to process. Understanding the root of this problem can also take a long time. Your loved one may dissolve into tears the first time her husband goes to work, or she may feel highly anxious watching her kids on a playground. Death becomes an enemy and she does not feel safe.

o   Remember Mother's and Father's Days, especially if your loved ones do not have living children. These days are very painful for many moms and dads whose children are not in their arms. If you are a pastor leading a church that recognizes moms on Mother's Day, consider encouraging women with babies in Heaven, women who have chosen an adoption plan for their child, and women who have experienced a failed adoption, to stand alongside the other mothers who can still hold their children. You will likely be shocked by the emotion-filled response you will receive. Most of these women suffer in silence and are easily forgotten on a day that forces them to remember the children they can no longer hold.

o Keep in mind that not all memories of their child will be sad and painful. Ask about the joyful moments.

o Offer to help scrapbook or build a memory shadow box for their child if they want one.

o Understand the child's first birthday in Heaven and the date of death anniversary (glory days) will be extremely painful. The couple will feel very conflicted in their emotions and confused as they anticipate these dates. New emotions will surface that they are unprepared for, as these huge milestones get closer.

o Remember anniversaries and contact your loved ones on these special days, *especially the first year*. Most people won't think to call. Others are fearful, thinking that if they make contact, they are only reminding the family about the tragedy that happened. Still others are unsure if the family wants to hear from anyone on these days. **Please call!**

The fact is that your loved ones are already thinking about the death of their child. They are secretly hoping that someone else is thinking of him or her too because that validates their child's life. Your loved ones are grieving and they are hurting. Silence will make them feel like they are alone and that people either don't care or don't remember; neither of which feel very good!

If your loved one's baby was born and died on the same day, consider referring to that day as, "their child's day." For instance, for our family, June 11th has become Kylie's Day. We celebrate her life by purchasing and wrapping up age-appropriate toys to donate to the Sunday school class that she would have been a part of. The kids in the class are always so excited to unwrap the gifts and play with the new toys and craft supplies. Four years later, our best friends also continue to send us flowers every June 11th, with a special note to let us know that they love us. Celebrating Kylie's life with these gifts and flowers are absolutely precious to me.

If your loved one's baby was born and died on different

days, remember birthdays and glory days, not just the first year but also every year. Most people won't!

<u>Specific Ways to Pray:</u>

- Pray for your loved one's salvation, if he or she does not already know Jesus as his or her personal Lord and Savior. I cannot imagine experiencing the death of a child, or the loss of a child through a failed adoption, without the strength of a relationship with God. It was my relationship with Jesus Christ that allowed me to find closure, peace, comfort, and the assurance that I would be reunited with my children in Heaven someday. I cannot even imagine how much more difficult it would have been to go through these tragic circumstances without Him!

- Pray that God will give the family wisdom and discernment to make the difficult decisions of possible surgeries to remove a child who has died in-utero (or in one of her tubes), whether to allow a miscarriage to take its natural course, any medications to use, birth control options, and post-partum medications if necessary.

- Pray for the decision-making process of any memorials or funerals. This can be very overwhelming, especially when a family had not even considered that they would have to be making these decisions at this time.

- Pray for the healing of your loved one as her body goes through the physical stages of recovering from pregnancy. With even mid-term losses, it is quite possible that she will begin to produce milk. This is a completely devastating physical and painful reminder that she does not have a child to feed.

- Pray that God would bring another woman to come alongside your loved one who has also experienced the loss of a child in a similar way, be it miscarriage, infant death, child death, or failed adoption.

- Pray for the spouse or significant other who may be getting overlooked during this time. He will be grieving the death of his child, even if he doesn't want to talk about it.

- Pray that God will give your loved ones the words to use to talk with any other children about the loss of a brother or sister. This can be devastating on so many levels for a family and sometimes finding the words to say that a child will understand can be so challenging.

- Pray that God will protect the heart of your loved one. Her emotions are on edge right now and she feels unsafe.

- Pray against Satan attacking your loved one's weaknesses.

- Pray for acceptance and closure, and for your loved ones to be able to work through the stages of grief in their own time.

- Pray for medical answers and that God will give doctors wisdom and discernment to understand what happened to cause the miscarriage, infant or child death, and if there is anything going on with the woman's body that needs further evaluation. Also pray that the doctors will use their best judgment to counsel the family of whether it is safe to continue bearing children, or if the best option is for the family to consider taking permanent measures to avoid future pregnancies.

- Pray that your loved ones will be able to find peace in their current circumstances.

- Pray that your loved ones will be able to find the courage and strength to get back into daily activities at their own pace.

- Pray against your loved one blaming herself for the death of her child.

- If your loved one becomes pregnant again, pray that God would give her strength to keep her heart in the right place. Pray against her fear that this child may also meet an early death.

- If your loved ones decide to pursue another adoption after a failed adoption, pray that they will not negatively transfer any feelings they may have into the next adoption.

- Pray that your loved ones will be able to see the heart and intent in well-intentioned (but perhaps hurtful) comments.

- Pray for your loved one's family and friends to be loving and supportive.

- Pray that your loved ones will be able to progress through their grief and work through any previous unresolved past hurt that may surface as a result of this loss.

*"Therefore encourage one another and build each other up,
just as in fact you are doing."*
—1 Thessalonians 5:11

Chapter Ten

Warning Signs

All this being said, do watch for warning signs. It is completely normal for a grieving person to feel overwhelmed, confused, frustrated, angry, disconnected, and depressed. These are all part of the grieving process to find healing through their pain and stages your loved ones will need to go through.

One of the best pieces of advice given to my husband shortly after Kylie's death was to understand that all of my feelings were normal and to expect my symptoms to fade slowly over time. If however, my husband did not see progress, or my grief continued to get worse after two months from the onset of the tragedy, my doctor wanted him to call. This would potentially indicate that my grieving was leading to clinical depression.

If it has been over two months since your loved one experienced the onset of their loss and they are showing no signs of improvement, please encourage them to seek professional help.

Here are things to look out for:

- Isolating themselves
- Constant discussions about death
- Inability to enjoy life
- Growing feelings of guilt and anger
- Major changes in sleep patterns
- Very low self-esteem and/or feeling worthless
- Loss of appetite and/or major weight loss
- Alcohol or drug abuse
- Neglecting their own care[14]

Please take any talk of suicide very seriously.
Call 911 and get professionals involved immediately.

At the end of this book, I also provide some great options of different resources that were tremendously helpful for our family while we were processing our grief. These organizations helped us to move forward from our losses when we were unsure of how to proceed and enabled us to understand that we were not alone. Hopefully, these organizations will prove to be great resources for your loved ones as well.

"Finally, brothers and sisters, whatever is true, whatever is noble, whatever is right, whatever is pure, whatever is lovely, whatever is admirable - if anything is excellent or praiseworthy - think about such things."
–Philippians 4:8

Chapter Eleven

Breaking It Down

There have been many days where I had to break down Philippians 4:8, in order to keep my own thoughts captive and to prevent a spiral of overwhelming emotions. I began practicing the following exercise when I was newly diagnosed with cancer at twenty-two years old. It has worked so well for me that I still work out many of my worries, stress, and anxiety, in this same way today.

I have found throughout the years that breaking down my stress biblically allows me to stay focused and grounded in God's Word. Doing this also gives me the gift of talking my worry and anxiety down, by focusing on the positive aspects of what is happening in the midst of my difficult circumstances. It allows me to stop focusing on everything that is scary and negative, while replacing my fear with peace.

This exercise is similar to pulling weeds in your yard. If you do not put grass seed (something good) in the hole where the weed was just removed, the weed is likely to grow back.

Using my very first bout with cancer, here is an actual example of how I talked down my worry and anxiety back in 1999. By encouraging your own loved ones to do this same exercise, you can use the Bible in a practical way to give your loved one a step-by-step solution to help lower their anxiety and stress.

Question: *What is "true" about my cancer?*

Answer: The doctors learned I have cancer. This is huge! Since we know I have cancer, we can do something about it. I have a lot of doctor's appointments, but every visit will eventually bring me closer to understanding how to fight this disease. My doctors and parents are being proactive. We are all looking for answers. While this cancer is unknown to me, God knows exactly what the problem is in my body and how to fix it. He created me and knows every cell in my body. He says that I am fearfully and wonderfully made (Psalm 139:14). Regardless of the outcome, my eternity is secure and I have Heaven to look forward to!

Question: *What is "noble" or honorable about my circumstances?*

Answer: I have some great doctors that are working very hard for me. I have a doctor who is willing to admit that he doesn't have all of the answers, but will do everything he can to find them. I have an incredible support system in my family, friends, and college professors who are continually supporting, encouraging, loving, and praying for me. My response to this cancer and my actions can become honorable when I choose to keep this trial in God's hands and use my circumstances to glorify Him.

Question: *What is "right" or just about this cancer?*

Answer: God is a loving and relational God. I do not believe that He "planned" or "purposed" for me to have this cancer, but I do believe that He allowed it to happen. This cancer is real and each doctor's appointment is leading me closer to the "right" or best treatment option. God desires obedience from me regardless of my circumstances. He will not leave me or forsake me as He promises in the book of Hebrews.

Question: *What is "pure" about this situation?*

Answer: I am young and still have many child-like tendencies in regards to perspectives of faith, life, and death. In the Bible, God asks us to become like little children and to have a child-like faith. I do not believe that death is the end of life, rather the beginning of an eternal, more intimate relationship with God in Heaven.

Question: *What is "lovely" about these circumstances?*

Answer: I have so many people praying for me and bringing this cancer before the throne of God. My volleyball teammates joke with me that I have new best friends at every school we play, since every other team in our conference knows my story. I am already seeing God encourage other people because I am choosing to be open about my circumstances. I am also seeing God use this cancer to build rapport with other cancer patients and even my radiation therapists. What a unique ministry that I never thought I would fit into so personally. God is using my cancer to encourage these women to re-evaluate their own personal relationships with Jesus Christ. There is no doubt in my mind that if I will allow it, God can use my cancer to share His love and compassion for other people.

Question: *What is admirable or good about this cancer?*

Answer: God desires to make me complete, not lacking anything, as I find in the book of James. He desires to use this awful cancer for good, for His glory. It is great that it appears we caught this cancer very early and even though it can be quite frustrating, it is good to leave no stone un-turned in searching for this disease. If there are tumors in other locations, they need to be dealt with appropriately so that they do not spread or get bigger. However, it is good news that so far no other procedure has been able to locate cancer cells anywhere else in my body. Ultimately, God is good and He desires to work all things, even this cancer, to show other people that He is worthy to be praised, even when bad things happen.

Question: *What is excellent and praiseworthy right now?*

Answer: The strength of God displayed in and through my life when I choose to live daily is incredible. By living daily, I find that I can have a joyful and content spirit through these circumstances because I am choosing not to worry about the future. If I am unable to do something about my cancer today, I will choose not to worry about it. By doing this, I do not deprive myself of my daily joy! I am also choosing to look at the positive aspects of life around me and have already listed over two hundred things that have made me smile in the last couple of weeks. Above all else, God is praiseworthy and I exist to serve Him.

"Truly I tell you, whatever you did for one of the least of these brothers and sisters of mine, you did for me."
–Matthew 25:40

Chapter Twelve

The Four Rules

I attempt to put these four rules into practice once I have given my initial condolences and offer to help:

1. I think before I speak and attempt to put myself in my loved ones shoes by asking myself:
   a. What would I want someone to say to me if I was going through this trial?
   b. Is what I am about to say helpful or potentially hurtful?
   c. Am I the most appropriate person to say what I think needs to be said?

2. If I am unable to say something helpful or I am not the right person to intervene, I send my loved one an e-mail or text message. I let them know I am praying for them, that I care, and that I am available if they need me. I also make sure that my current contact information is in the email, just so that everything is in one place for him or her, and they do not need to search for my phone number.

3. I ask how our family can provide tangible support and I take action. I go into these conversations, already having ideas of what the family might need. Often times, this means cooking meals, ordering food for delivery (if the family is not local to where I am currently living), taking care of their children, offering to run errands, and being available to talk when they are ready.

4. During the first month, I check back weekly, offering to help out as needed. During the next two months, I call or e-mail every other week, unless they come to me for support. I do my best to write down commitments I've made, remission days, anniversaries, due dates, birthdays, glory days, and any other important days that I need to remember on my calendar.

I want to make sure that I am praying for the family on these specific days and the days leading up to these events. I will also call or e-mail to let my loved ones know I am thinking of and praying for them on the days that I know will be difficult for them. However, if I do not write these dates down on my calendar immediately, my own life gets in the way and I tend to forget!

"Be completely humble and gentle; be patient, bearing with one another in love."
–Ephesians 4:2

Chapter Thirteen

The Oasis

I hear the word "oasis" and envision a place of peace and serenity in a desolate and dry desert. My trial is that desert, the dirt road, my journey.

As I move forward, I look back and see miles of dusty roads where bags have been left behind. These bags are parts of my grief that I have already been able to let go of.

I look to my left and right and see my closest family and friends, carrying more bags—my burdens. They are providing me with consistent and intentional love as they walk beside me through the treacherous terrain. I am able to relax a little bit more, but still feel unprepared for the journey. My head is spinning with information I don't know how to process. I feel emotionally dizzy.

I look forward, realizing I am slowly walking toward a beautiful sandy beach with crystal blue water and palm trees. I immediately reject what I see as a mirage, because I no longer believe a place like this exists.

My loved ones understand and know I am not ready. They do not pressure me or belittle the road I have already traveled. They do not attempt to convince me that what I see is real—they will allow me to get there on my own time, when I am ready. They encourage my progress, seeing how far I've already come, as they've walked beside me this entire journey. Some days I have moved forward quickly; others days I have stayed put, or even backtracked.

They tell me, "It's okay!"

Their love and grace help keep me grounded and give me clarity, even through my roughest days.

I don't deserve it.

I feel thankful.

Erica McNeal

I continue to watch the bags drop as we move forward—this makes me smile. It's been a long time since I've really smiled and it feels good.

I look ahead at the oasis again, this time with a glimmer of hope. Maybe it could be real!

I think of the road I've already traveled and the long conversations I've had along the way.

I begin to believe.

Peace and healing are calling out to me.

I still have a lot of baggage, but the sign ahead says, "Come as you are!" There is no need for me to deal with every emotion right now.

I need to just take one step at a time.

My loved ones have created a safe haven for me, something to look forward to—the very oasis we are walking toward. A place where I can be myself, let go of my fears, talk through my pain, and work through my grief; a place where I am free from judgment, where people want to help me get to the heart of my struggles. My family and friends have created the very essence of this beauty emanating up ahead.

I have been walking in this desert for too long.

I look forward, this time with excitement.

A few more bags drop to the ground.

The weight of my burdens becomes lighter. The oasis is no longer a mirage in my mind, but a real place—something that has been created just for me.

I am ready.

It is time!

I can finally face my difficult circumstances and deal with my emotions.

I take a deep breath and step onto the fine, soft sand. It is warm. The crystal blue water is beckoning me. And the chairs show me that my loved ones are ready to help me find rest.

They are even ready to sit with me in silence, if that is what I need.

There is no better place for me to work through the depths of my grief, than surrounded by those who love me most.

While my family and friends have created and led me to this oasis, perhaps somehow, some way, they can become a part of my ability to find beauty and purpose in the road that led us here!

"Love is patient, love is kind. It does not envy, it does not boast, it is not proud. It is not rude, it is not self-seeking, it is not easily angered, it keeps no record of wrongs. Love does not delight in evil but rejoices with the truth. It always protects, always trusts, always hopes, always perseveres. Love never fails."
−1 Corinthians 13:4-8

Chapter Fourteen

Conclusion

People who are suffering need to know they are loved and cared for. Confidence is built to share their emotions and feelings when you are willing to walk through their entire journey. Loving someone who is grieving takes practice and an investment on your part—it is challenging on so many levels.

There will be many ups and downs on the roller coaster of emotions when dealing with loss. Please do not expect to drop in and out of the journey when it is convenient for you and still be able to speak truth into their lives—they are not likely going to trust you. Those who are suffering need consistency and a safe place to work through their deepest, darkest fears, and emotions. In their desperate need to move forward from their pain, often times a person struck with grief will disengage with anyone they feel is holding them back, or continues to discount their tragic circumstances, their feelings, or their grieving process.

The greatest gift given to us during our deepest grief was the stability of those who loved us most. I needed my closest family and friends to be the only ones to speak truth into my life when my reality was distorted. Through their reliability, a deep trust was developed for me to share the depths of my soul, no matter how ugly it was. And, let me tell you, it got ugly! With this small group of people, I feared no judgment, but knew that they would gently rebuke and guide me when needed.

My journey of grief was confusing and frustrating. Only those who were consistent in our lives could understand the truth, versus moments of venting, to see the progress we made, and to help us move forward from our pain.

These suggestions are by no means exhaustive, but will hopefully give you a good starting place to care for your loved one.

By learning from others, both the good and the bad, my hope is that you can use these suggestions to provide an incredible support system for your loved one.

When you stay consistent and intentional, you create a beautiful oasis in a very dry desert for your loved one to grieve appropriately.

References

Chapter 1
[1] http://www.pregnancy-info.net/premature_baby.html.
[2] http://www.mayomedicallaboratories.com/test-catalog/print.php?unit_code=57151.

Chapter 7
[3] http://www.studylight.org/com/mhc-com/view.cgi?book=1co&chapter=010
[4] Jeremiah 29:11, King James Version
[5] http://www.studylight.org/com/mhc-com/view.cgi?book=jer&chapter=029.
[6] Genesis 3:17.

Chapter 8
[7] Luke 22:42
[8] Luke 22:44
[9] www.cancer.gov.
[10] http://locksoflove.org/.
[11] An incredible Christian Comedian to consider listening to or watching, is Ken Davis. His wife Diane, is also a cancer survivor and they both do everything they can to live fully alive! You can find his website here: www.kendavis.com.
[12] http://carm.org/chronological-development-of-a-baby.

Chapter 9
[13] www.webmd.com

Chapter 11

[14] http://www.focusonthefamily.com/lifechallenges/emotional_health/depression.aspx

Resources for Hurting Families

The views expressed in Good Grief! are solely those of the author and do not necessarily reflect the views or endorsement of the following organizations. These resources proved tremendously helpful for our family by showing us how to move forward from our losses, while reminding us that we were not alone.

Christian-Based Ministries:

Focus on the Family: www.focusonthefamily.com
Grief Share: www.griefshare.org
Rest Ministries: www.restministries.org

Cancer:

American Cancer Society: www.cancer.org
Cancer Care: www.cancercare.org

Child-Loss:

Faces of Loss: www.facesofloss.com
Grieve Out Loud: www.grieveoutloud.org

*All resources were listed with permission.

Endorsement and Support Websites

Kevin Baker: www.martharoadbaptist.org

Tom Dawson: www.fbcofallon.com

Ken and Diane Davis: www.kendavis.com

Dr. Joseph Grana: www.hiu.edu

Jodie Guerrero: www.jodiesjourney.com

Sean McDowell: www.seanmcdowell.org

Dr. Doug Munton: www.fbcofallon.com

Tommy Nelson: www.songofsolomon.com

Drs. Les and Leslie Parrot: www.lesandleslie.com

Jen Rumley: www.therumleys.blogspot.com

Alice Sullivan (Editor): www.alicesullivan.com

Lt Col Matthew Vann: www.matvann37.blogspot.com

WestBow Press (Publisher): www.westbowpress.com

About the Author

Erica McNeal is a military wife and stay at home mom with fifteen years of experience in Youth, Marriage, and Women's Ministries. A graduate of Hope International University, in Fullerton, CA, Erica received her B.A. in Church Ministry, and has used this degree working in both part and full time ministry positions. Erica has also shared her life experiences as a guest speaker in ten different states to churches, women's groups, and military leadership groups.

Erica's vision is to challenge the Christian line that states God will not give us more than we can handle because she believes that God will allow us to be stretched beyond our human capabilities in order to show us our need for Him, to deepen our faith, and to show us that HIS strength is limitless!

Erica resides wherever the Air Force takes her family, with her husband Todd and two children.

Website: www.ericamcneal.com
Twitter: @toddanderica

CPSIA information can be obtained at www.ICGtesting.com
Printed in the USA
LVOW090159240412

278815LV00002B/4/P